Ashes
into
Gold

Ashes
into
Gold

The Journey of Spirituality

Martin M. Davis

WINEPRESS **WP** PUBLISHING

Packaged by WinePress Publishing, PO Box 428, Enumclaw, WA 98022. The views expressed or implied in this work do not necessarily reflect those of WinePress Publishing. The author(s) is ultimately responsible for the design, content and editorial accuracy of this work.

ISBN 1-57921-755-9
Library of Congress Catalog Card Number: 2004094225

TO SARA

Table of Contents

A Personal Note from the Author

Writing this book has been a long and difficult process. Not because the words were difficult to put on paper, although that is always hard enough, but because the *living* of what is written in this book has been difficult. Years ago, my friend and fellow therapist Ken Gilburth warned me: "Be careful what you write; you will have to live it." He was right!

I began to formulate the ideas for this book at a time when I thought I understood the journey that we will come to know in the pages to follow as *the journey of spirituality* through the wilderness of change and growth. To be sure, at that time I had indeed learned much about the journey through reading, formal education, and more than forty years of personal experience, and I was able to communicate many truths about the journey not only in writing, but also in counseling and conducting seminars. Furthermore, I had learned much about wandering in the wilderness of change and growth from the many clients I had been privileged to work with in my years as a therapist, both in private practice and with the counseling ministry of a large evangelical Christian church.

Nevertheless, God intended for me to personally live out what is written in this book, at a level I had never before experienced. In one memorable summer, God began to address me directly in "big dreams," as Carl Jung described those dreams that portend significant events in our lives, and in repeated encounters with others—sometimes total strangers—who took me by the arm and assured (warned?) me that the Holy Spirit was about to work in my life. Now, years later, I can fully appreciate the words in the New Testament that warn: "It is a dreadful thing to fall into the hands of the living God" (Heb. 10:31).

Shortly after my dreams and encounters with those messengers of God, I separated from my wife, and, at my insistence—as well as my deep regret—we subsequently divorced (by the grace of God, we are now remarried). Quite unintentionally, and not in the least in accordance with my plans, I then began a deep descent into ashes that led me to the depths of clinical depression and utter despair. I experienced fear, anxiety, and an overwhelming sense of loneliness unlike anything I had ever experienced, even in those days, years ago, when I struggled with addiction to alcohol. To make matters worse, within a few months my mother died, and I experienced the loss not only of a parent, but of a true friend. By then, I was truly wandering in the wilderness—and was thoroughly lost. To ease the incredible pain I felt, I sought security and meaning in relationships, and invested in others much energy that would have been better given to God. I learned how easily we make idols of relationships; I also learned what poor substitutes they are for a relationship with God. During my continued wandering in the wilderness, I studied Zen for several years and found much of value there. I met many wonderful people through that experience, many of whom were burnt out Christians who, in some sense, had been let down by the version of the faith they had been taught. I finally realized, however, that, at least for me, Zen was a dead end. Whereas Zen offered karma, Christianity

offered grace, and I was sorely in need of the latter. I tried lib-
eral Christianity, but soon learned that without the Virgin Birth,
the Incarnation, the Atonement, and a literal—yes, it really happened!—Resurrection, there really wasn't much left that could
be called Christianity. With the help of C.S. Lewis, I realized I
needed my Christianity full strength, not the insipid, watered-
down version offered by far too many churches today. Finally,
after many years in the wilderness, wrestling with God, I returned to my conservative, evangelical Christian roots and renewed my relationship with the loving Father who had been
waiting for me all along with open arms. I also renewed my
relationship with the only woman who has ever loved me unconditionally: my wife, Sara.

Today, I am beginning to learn what it is like to live in the
promised land. I do not intend to imply, however, that all my
difficulties are behind me, for living in the promised land, like
living in the wilderness, also poses its challenges, difficulties,
and peculiar encounters with God. Nor do I intend to portray
myself as an expert on the journey of spirituality; I know better!
But I have learned a little, and I hope to share some of that
learning with you.

So I do not write as an expert, but as a fellow traveler on the
journey of spirituality. To be sure, there are few experts on this
subject (although some of the great saints may qualify as experts, though they would never say so). I believe that, in light of
eternity and the greatness of God, we are all really just begin-
ners on the spiritual path.

Therefore, the book you are reading today is very different
from the book I started—and thought I had finished—years
ago. My thoughts and ideas have been tempered and refined in
the heat of the wilderness experience, and much of the original
text of this book has been revised. What I once knew through
formal education, reading, personal experience, and the experiences of others, I have now learned through deeper and more

painful first-hand experience. Today, I do not claim to be a better man, only a deeper one.

In addition, I believe that much of what is written here is sorely needed in the marketplace of ideas that has become the big business of Christian publishing. A relationship with God is not all light and victory (although it will culminate in that one day). As we shall see in the pages to follow, a relationship with God has many varied aspects: some wonderful, delightful, and pleasant; others painful, difficult, and even frightening. Much has been written about the more pleasant aspects of a relationship with God, and that is as it should be; for we are made for relationship with our Creator, and our greatest fulfillment, both now and in the life to come, is nurtured in that relationship. Nevertheless, there are also difficulties in a relationship with God, and I have not glossed over them in this book. To be sure, the journey of spirituality is not always a leisurely stroll atop the sun-lit peaks of spiritual experience, but is sometimes a grinding, slogging ordeal trod step by trudging step through the muddy lowlands of the spiritual valley.

In conclusion: Now that you know something of my journey through the wilderness of change and growth, you may rest assured that when I describe the pain of those who are drowning deep within the well of desperation, I know whereof I speak. You may also rest assured that when I say God will turn *your* ashes into gold, I also know whereof I speak. First, however, it is your worthy task to accept his invitation to join him in the wilderness of change and growth and therein be transformed by the living God.

If you find yourself in the ash pile of life, I trust that this book will offer you encouragement and hope. Believe it or not, there is a way out of the ashes, though not an easy one. There is hope, though it can be difficult to see in the darkness. You are invited to enter the wilderness of change and growth, wherein you may encounter God. I assure you, there is a promised land, and God will guide you to it. But first, there is the wilderness.

Preface

The book you are about to read describes a journey, one that each of us, at some point in our lives, is called to undertake. We will come to know the journey described in the pages to follow as *the journey of spirituality*, a difficult pilgrimage that takes us through the wilderness of change and growth.

As we shall see, the journey of spirituality often begins in the ash pile of life, that painful place of descent wherein we may find ourselves after we have undergone a major life-changing event. That event may be divorce, the loss of a job or career, the loss of a loved one, or the discovery of a terminal illness. Or we may descend into ashes as a result of ongoing events or circumstances that have come to characterize our lives. Those who are overwhelmed by addiction, held captive in abusive relationships, trapped in meaningless jobs or careers, or who suffer debilitating illnesses are invited to enter the wilderness of change and growth and therein encounter God. In short, this book is for all whose hopes, dreams, and plans lie in ashes at their feet.

The journey of spirituality in the wilderness of change and growth is one that leads from pain and brokenness to psychological, emotional, and spiritual wholeness. Therefore, whether you have yet to begin your journey, or have been traveling for some time, this book is for you.

In the pages to come, you are invited to follow the path of others who have embarked on the journey of spirituality, and from their experiences you may learn what lies ahead as you embark on your journey.

Moreover, you will have the opportunity to explore spirituality at great length. Rather than an otherworldly state that one seeks to attain, spirituality is herein understood as a *process* of psychological, emotional, and spiritual growth. This process is described in this book as the journey of spirituality through the wilderness of change and growth. The spiritual principles outlined in this book are for everyone, because all of us—whether we choose to heed the call or not—are invited to enter the wilderness of change and growth, wherein we may encounter God.

While this book is written from a Christian perspective, the spiritual principles addressed herein are universal and apply to those who practice other traditions, for the Holy Bible—God's word in written form—speaks eloquently to the human condition in all places and times. Furthermore, the principles described herein, as well as much of the language used, will be intimately familiar to those who participate in Twelve Step programs or other self-help groups that have a spiritual foundation. Familiar concepts such as faith and surrender are discussed at length, for the spiritual journey of change and growth necessarily entails faith in, as well as surrender to, a higher power. For me, the true higher power, and the one who guides my own spiritual journey, is Jesus Christ.

I invite all of you who have experienced the ashes of life to embark upon the journey of spirituality through the wilderness of change and growth. On the other side of that place of trial, testing, and transformation, you will find waiting the promised land flowing with milk and honey.

Acknowledgments

Anyone who spends a few years wandering through the wilderness of change and growth is bound to meet a few interesting characters along the way. In fact, the great stories and myths assure us that, at the various crossroads on our journeys, helpers will appear to point us in the right direction and, perhaps, even walk a little way with us.

One of those helpers on my journey has been my friend and fellow therapist Ken Gilburth. Ken acted as a guide during the early days of my wandering through the wilderness of change and growth. Ken helped me to understand that the events and problems of our lives are not the meaningless, mundane occurrences of what some call ordinary existence—or worse, quiet desperation—but are, in fact, the replaying of great stories that embody universal truths. Without Ken Gilburth, this book could never have been written. My respect and appreciation for him is evidenced by my quoting him several times in the pages to follow.

Another helper who guided me a little further on the journey of spirituality is Clare Van Lent, the director of the Dwelling Place, a Franciscan prayer center in my state. To me, Clare is the embodiment of the life of faith, for she demonstrates in her daily life what it means to live by faith, not by sight. While there are many who talk the talk, Clare is one who walks the walk. Her guidance and counsel helped me through some difficult places on the path. We will meet Clare again in the pages to come.

There are many others who have taught me much about life in the wilderness of change and growth. They have shared their stories with me in the therapist's office. I refer to the clients I have been privileged to serve in my years as a therapist, both in private practice and with the counseling ministry of a large evangelical Christian church. Much of what has been written in this book is simply what I have learned from them. Some of them appear, incognito, in the pages to follow. I have great respect for those who are willing to struggle and grow through the counseling process. What great courage they have! From having sat in both chairs, I know how easy it is to be the therapist, and how difficult it is to be the client.

I would like to thank Ron Halvorson of RPI Publishing, Inc. Ron provided the impetus that enabled me to finally finish writing this book. Ron also read the final manuscript and encouraged me to continue this project. He also offered valuable insights that allowed me to clarify certain aspects of the text as they relate to the journey of spirituality.

Moreover, I would like to acknowledge members of my own family who have played a part in the writing and publishing of this book. First, I would like to acknowledge my parents, both of whom have passed away in recent years. Their passing has been part of my struggle in the wilderness. My mother, Billie, and my father, Martin Sr., would both be very pleased to see this book in print and to know that one of their five children had written it.

I would also like to acknowledge Ken and Hilda Courtney. One of the more joyous aspects of my journey in recent years has been the restoration of my relationship with Ken and my sister Hilda, after we had drifted apart for many years. I have gained much understanding about the beauty and wisdom of God's design for the family by watching and learning from Ken and Hilda as they relate to their children and grandchildren. Ken is a man whose life is founded upon a deep and abiding love of God. I have never known a man who, I believe, loves God more than does Ken Courtney. His mansion in heaven will be a large one. Ken was one of the first to read the final manuscript of this book. His enthusiastic response to the message contained in these pages was evidenced by his desire to participate in the publishing of this work. Because of his belief in the ministry this book could bring to those who need it, Ken, along with his wife Hilda, made the publishing of this book possible.

Finally, and far from least, I must acknowledge and thank my wife, Sara. She has unfailingly believed in me and stood by me for more than twenty years, even during a painful time when I was far from her. In order for me to have the time to write and complete the assignments God has given me, sacrifices have been necessary. While it is one thing for me to make sacrifices in order to accomplish what I believe God has called me to do, it is quite another to ask someone else to sacrifice alongside me. Yet, Sara has been willing to make whatever sacrifices are necessary for our writing ministry to become a reality. My journey has taught me that a woman like Sara is a rare treasure. As the book of Proverbs states: "A wife of noble character who can find? She is worth far more than rubies" (Prov. 31:10). To be sure, it is a rare and uncommon privilege for a man to be loved unconditionally; yet Sara, who knows me better than anyone ever has, loves me unconditionally. Because of her unending faith and support, as well as her willingness to accept, without complaint, my crazy way of life, I gratefully dedicate this book to her.

—Martin M. Davis
Jackson, Mississippi
Spring, 2004

Introduction

O*NCE UPON A TIME* there was a soldier, a bright young officer, who stood proudly at attention in his shiny-buttoned uniform, a colorful plume in his tall officer's hat. The gallant young lieutenant served an ambitious king who sought many lands to rule; thus, the future was bright for soldiers.

One day, the ambitious king died, and a new, peace-loving king took the throne of the land; hence, there was no longer any need for soldiers. Therefore, the shiny young officer was discharged from the army. Because he had no craft but soldiering, he quickly became poor and hungry. Broken and in despair, he went into a deep, dark forest.

Deep in the woods, the soldier met a wrinkled old man—the devil. "Why are you wandering alone in the forest, poor and destitute?" asked the devil. The soldier replied, "I have recently been discharged from the army, and I have no craft but soldiering." The devil laughed cunningly and said, "Then come with me, and I will give you work." The soldier happily agreed. "But," said the devil with an ominous tone in his voice, "I warn you: You must serve me for seven years, and during that time you may not cut your hair, shave your beard, or trim your nails. At the end of seven years, I will pay you in full." The soldier did not like the bargain at all, but because he was poor, hungry, and destitute, he agreed to the devil's harsh terms. Then, the devil took the soldier into a dark cave, wherein they descended a deep stairway to hell.

The soldier was assigned the task of tending the fires beneath the cauldrons where the souls of the damned were boiling. At first the work was hot and difficult in the dimly lit surroundings, but soon the soldier took to it readily enough. Much of his time was spent shoveling away the ashes that quickly accumulated around the cauldrons from the great amount of wood the fires required. The time passed quickly for the soldier, so that when his seven years were finished, he felt as though he had been in hell only half a year.

At the end of the seven years, the devil came to release the soldier from his servitude, as had been agreed. As the soldier prepared to leave hell, he asked the devil for his wages. To the soldier's dismay, the devil paid him with seven bags full of ashes— the same ashes the soldier had shoveled for seven years. The soldier was disheartened and deeply disappointed to end up with nothing but ashes; but having no power over the devil, he accepted his wages and, step by trudging step, climbed the stairway that ascended from hell.

When he came into the sunshine, the soldier was saddened to see his uniform soiled, tattered, and torn, its buttons tarnished with age. He realized how grimy he had become from his years of shoveling ashes and tending the fires of hell. He longed for a bath, for he was weary of the dirty ashes that covered his skin. Also, he wanted to trim his hair, beard, and nails and rest on a clean, soft bed. So he journeyed forth, even though he did not know where he was going.

Only a short way into his journey, the tattered soldier came upon a stream that bordered a dark and mysterious forest. Because the brook was swollen with the melting snow of early spring, he could see no way across. Thus, he put down his bags of ashes, removed his knapsack from across his shoulder, and sat down upon a mossy log to rest.

As he tarried by the swirling stream, the soldier grew uneasy because he heard strange and frightening sounds coming from the forest beyond. In addition, he began to think of the danger he risked if he tried to ford the heavily swollen stream; he feared he would be washed away and drowned. As he grew more fearful at the prospects of continuing his journey, he began to regret having come to such a mysterious place; he even thought of returning to hell, for though the work there was hot and dirty, at least the surroundings were familiar, unlike this strange place full of danger and frightening noises. He determined not to go back, however, for he knew that no matter how much he labored in hell, he would only receive more ashes.

As the soldier sat upon the log, pondering what to do, his thoughts wandered back to the childhood prayers his mother taught him years before in the nursery of their small cottage in a distant valley. Then he remembered the wise words of his grandfather, who taught him that Providence never failed to lend a helping hand to those who asked. Thus, with some discomfort because of his lack of practice, the soldier removed his crumpled hat, cleared his throat, and quietly voiced a simple prayer to the heavens, asking for deliverance from the impasse that faced him.

After a humble amen, the soldier gathered his courage, arose, and surveyed the stream's swirling currents. Suddenly, he felt the wind rise as it rushed past his face and lifted the hair from his shoulders. He noticed the branches in the trees beginning to wave and heard the leaves swirling and cartwheeling across the ground as the wind grew stronger. Then he heard the cracking and creaking of a huge dead oak that broke from the top and fell crashing to the ground, bridging the stream not far from where he stood. With great apprehension, the soldier moved closer and surveyed the sight before him. Because the tree was severely decayed, the soldier was not certain the trunk would support his weight as he walked upon it. Nevertheless, since there was no other way across the swollen stream, he offered a simple prayer of faith to the heavens and set foot upon the rotting trunk. As he hurried safely to the far side of the brook, the decayed oak sagged in the middle, then groaned as it broke in half and tumbled into the water below. With a trembling hand, the soldier wiped his brow as he looked heavenward and breathed a sigh of gratitude for his safe passage across the roaring stream. Then he made his way into the mysterious, dark forest.

As the soldier entered the forest, he used his rusty old sword to clear the brush and heavy undergrowth from his path, for these woods were strange and rarely explored, and there was no clearly defined trail. Because the journey was difficult, he soon grew weary with hunger. As he felt inside one pocket of his coat and then another, he was saddened to learn that he had no more food. When he had left hell, he had taken only the bags of ashes and a small knapsack in which there was little room for food as well as the few belongings he had salvaged. As the ache in his stomach worsened, he began to think of his days in hell. He remembered the warm bowl of soup he received each evening at the end of a long day of labor. As the hunger gnawed deep inside, he longed to sit by the cauldrons eating his soup, for surely that was better than the aching that tormented him now. Growing weaker with each step, the soldier feared that his journey was soon to end, for he could not last much longer without food.

As he continued to trudge through the forest, the soldier suddenly noticed a strange bush ahead, one covered with magic berries. Gaining strength at the sight, he hurried to the bush bedecked with the enchanting, deeply colored fruit. Then, he picked some of the berries and tasted them. To his delight, he found they were delicious, and so he ate until he was full. After eating as much as he could hold, the soldier removed his knapsack from across his shoulder so that he could fill it with berries to take with him as he traveled on. To his surprise, however, there were no more berries on the bush; there had been only enough to fill him up. Nevertheless, having regained both his strength and his hope, the soldier determined to continue his journey, praying that he would find another bush covered with magic berries in the forest ahead.

The soldier spent many days wandering through the forest. At first he had been able to keep track of the passing days by making a scratch on a small piece of rawhide that hung from his knapsack, one mark for each day in the forest. Yet the rawhide had long since become covered with scratches, and the soldier had lost count of the number of days he had journeyed from hell. Oftentimes, the soldier yearned to be free of the dark woods in which he had traveled for so long, for there were always frightening beasts about, and the work of hacking his way through the forest was often difficult. In the winter, when the snow covered the ground and he shook with cold, the soldier longed to sip a cup of hot tea and sit by the hearth before a warm fire. At other times, he longed for a feather bed to rest upon, one piled high with layers of warm quilts to insulate him from the cold. When he dwelled upon those things he lacked in the forest, he would think of returning to hell, for at least it was warm by the cauldrons, and there was always hot soup to eat at the end of a long day. Nevertheless, as he rubbed the thick calluses that had grown upon his hands from years of shoveling ashes in hell, the grimy soldier determined to go forward, for he felt himself being gently drawn onward, and he could not help but believe that something better lay ahead than the hell he had left behind.

One day, the soldier stopped to lean against a tree so he could remove his boots and rub his feet as they had begun to ache from the many miles he had walked that day. As he rubbed the sores and calluses on his tired feet, he began to think of the many days he had wandered in the forest and how he had often yearned to be free of these deep woods. With a sigh and a nod, he realized that his complaining about the ever-present underbrush as well as his yearning to escape the forest had done him no good; it had only made his journey more difficult. As his realization deepened, he began to understand that, instead of flowing with the currents of life, he was fighting against them and, thereby, creating a hell almost as real as the one he had left behind. Closing his eyes and bowing his head with an attitude of humble acceptance, he solemnly pledged to trust his path to the wisdom of the divine Providence his grandfather had told him about many years before.

As the days came and went, the soldier began to notice with amused delight that his life seemed different since he had decided to let go of his own will and intentions and trust his life to the heavens. Nowadays, when his vision was especially clear, the forest seemed almost like a home to him, for he loved the sight of the graceful, bounding deer and the laughter of the misty waterfalls hidden in green, mossy hollows, blessings his time in the wilderness was teaching him to notice and treasure. And though he sometimes grew lonely, he had the lovely mountain laurel and the many-colored meadow flowers to brighten his way. Even more, he was especially grateful that he had never grown hungry in the forest since he had first discovered the bush covered with magic berries; for each day since, he had stumbled upon another bush whose fruit sustained him for another day. As he reflected upon many things, the soldier thanked the heavens for the many gifts the forest offered, and he realized that, even in this place, he had learned much about peace and contentment.

One day, at a time when he no longer thought so often about leaving the forest, the soldier's path opened into the bright sunshine, and suddenly he could see for miles in many directions. Then he spotted a secluded inn nestled high in an alpine meadow. He made his way through sweet grass laced with the blue, yellow, pink, and white wild flowers of late summer and drew near the strangely peaceful dwelling. As his eyes scanned the lovely gardens that surrounded the inn, he was delighted by the fragrant scents that filled the air, borne by the gentle breezes that wafted across the many varieties of roses that grew there. Strange trees and unusual shrubs stood in the garden and added a sense of mystery to the paradisiacal setting. Because he knew nothing of this unusual place, the soldier removed his crumpled hat and, with lowly demeanor, slowly walked inside, his long coarse hair tumbling about his shoulders.

Upon entering the inn, the soldier spotted the innkeeper who was humming cheerfully as he polished the heavy oak desk on which the guest register lay. The ashy, grimy soldier, hat in hand, approached the innkeeper, cleared his throat, and humbly asked for a room and a bath. The innkeeper greeted him kindly and extended a callused, scarred hand in welcome. Suddenly, the soldier realized he had no money or nothing of value to offer his host; all he possessed for his seven years of labor in hell were seven bags full of ashes. The innkeeper noticed the worried, weary look in the soldier's eyes. "What troubles you, pilgrim?" he asked. The soldier replied, "I have nothing with which to pay for my room and bath." The innkeeper smiled knowingly at the haggard, tired traveler and said with a wink, "Reach your hand into one of the bags you carry." Not understanding, but not knowing what else to do, the soldier reached his hand into one of the bags. Much to his surprise, he discovered that his ashes had turned into gold.

CHAPTER 1

Descent into Ashes

But those who suffer he delivers in their suffering; he speaks to them in their affliction.

—The Book of Job

A UNIVERSAL HUMAN DRAMA

C ertain themes occur repeatedly in folklore, fairy tales, and classical mythology. These themes are universal; that is, they are part of the human drama in all places through all times. Therefore, these themes run like vital threads through the fabric of our own lives.

One of these important themes is the "descent into ashes." In fairy tales and folklore, ashes represent a "sooty, depressed, 'out of it' time" of sorrow and suffering.[1] Cinderella, the cinders or ashes girl, was a scullery maid who cleaned the hearth, washed the dishes, and slaved down on her knees, scrubbing the floor for her abusive stepmother and her debutante sisters. In the ancient story *Iron John*, popularized by Robert Bly, the youthful son of the king descended into ashes by taking a dirty job as a cook's helper, carrying wood and water and raking the cinders around the hearth in the basement kitchen of a distant castle. In the opening story of the present book, the young soldier descended into the underworld and spent his days shoveling the ashes around the cauldrons of hell.

The universal drama of descent into ashes is not only a recurring theme in fairy tales and folklore, but is also a theme that recurs in many stories recorded in the Holy Bible. In the Old Testament story of Job, the descent into ashes is portrayed in dramatic fashion. After his many children were killed in a violent storm and all his vast possessions and properties had been destroyed, the once-prosperous Job sat in a pile of ashes for weeks, scraping the sores that had arisen on his body and mourning the loss of his family as he struggled to understand the tragedy that had become his life. The Old Testament also recounts the story of Joseph, an arrogant boy whose descent into the ash pile of sorrow and suffering began when he was thrown into a dry well by his jealous older brothers. Later, Joseph was sold into slavery and taken to Egypt, where, eventually, he was put in prison. From these ancient stories we learn that the descent into ashes is a time of pain, sorrow, and great suffering.

MANY ROADS LEAD DOWN

These ancient narratives, however, describe only a few of the avenues that lead down into the ashes of life. To be sure, there are other roads that lead down, for the descent into ashes may be taken by many routes. Some have descended into ashes as a result of a devastating accident. Joni Eareckson Tada, a noted Christian author and speaker, descended into ashes as a teenager when she dove into the water and broke her neck. Today, she remains paralyzed from the neck down. Others have descended into ashes because of a debilitating illness. Dave Dravecky, the strong young athlete who lost his pitching arm to cancer, descended into ashes when the disease destroyed his career as a professional baseball player. Others have descended into ashes because of social and political injustice. The famous Russian dissident Alexander Solzhenitsyn, author of *The Gulag Archipelago*, descended into ashes when he was cast into the seemingly hopeless degradation of a Communist slave camp.

Many others have descended into ashes in less dramatic but more common fashion. Divorce, a heart-wrenching descent accompanied by devastating pain and heartache for all involved, is a well-worn path into the ash pile of life. Unemployment takes many down into the sooty realm of ashes. The sixty-year-old executive fired from a life-long career soon after the arrival of a young boss with new ideas knows the suffocating feeling of descent. Depression, a physical-emotional disorder known as the common cold of psychiatry, takes millions in our society spiraling downward. Addiction is a common road that leads many in our society into ashes. In Alcoholics Anonymous, addiction is described as an elevator that goes only one direction: down. One who walks into his first A.A. meeting and says, "My name is Chris; I'm an alcoholic," knows he has gone down into ashes. Like the alcoholic, the bright young lawyer who snorts away her license and her future because of her captivity to cocaine understands the descent into ashes. The compulsive gambler who loses his home and family knows the taste of ashes when he takes yet another meal at the rescue mission. Moreover, the battered wife whose dependency chains her to an abusive husband knows the ashen feel of enslavement. And the popular, tearful, but clandestinely promiscuous televangelist caught with the prostitute also understands the depth of the descent into ashes.

Like Icarus, the arrogant youth of Greek mythology who flew too near the sun, we all eventually plummet downward and experience the ashes side of life: the dark, grimy, sooty realm of sorrow and suffering. Those who have practiced the spiritual principles known as the Twelve Steps know that Step One is the ashes step: we admit that we are powerless, that at least in some sense, our lives have become unmanageable. This step is simply a way of saying that our wings have melted, that we have descended from the sunny, happier realm of life, and have crashed, tangled and torn, into the ash heap of "pain, brokenness, and human limitation."[2]

Rising from the Ashes

The descent into ashes, however, is not merely a time of meaningless hardship and suffering; it is also the beginning of a transitional period, a time of metamorphosis when, like the mythical phoenix, something old dies and something new rises in its place. Myth, folklore, fairy tales, and most importantly, the sacred texts of the Holy Bible teach the universal truth that the sooty, depressed time in the ashes of life is, for many of us, a prerequisite to the healing, change, and growth that leads to psychological, emotional, and spiritual wholeness.[3] After her time as the ashes maid, Cinderella—not her arrogant and spoiled sisters—won the heart of the charming prince and spent her remaining days in the palace. After shoveling the ashes around the hearth in the basement kitchen of a distant castle, the golden-haired son of the king in the story of *Iron John* grew from youthful naiveté to mature manhood and future kingship. Following his descent into the ash pile of suffering and sorrow, Job built a new family and regained his fortune. After his time of slavery and imprisonment, the once-arrogant Joseph grew to become the wise and insightful prime minister of Egypt.

Therefore, ashes represent not only a time of sorrow, suffering, and brokenness, but also the beginning of a requisite time of transition that is marked by significant growth and change and followed by eventual restoration and healing. As seen in the stories of Cinderella, the son of the king in *Iron John*, the gallant young soldier who descended into hell, and in the stories of Job and Joseph, the descent into ashes is the beginning of a painful but essential metamorphosis, a vital time wherein ashes begin to be transformed into gold.

ROOTED IN ASHES

We may gain greater insight into the meaning of the descent into ashes by considering two very dissimilar kinds of trees: the oak and the palm. Before the oak can grow to maturity and provide acorns for animals, shelter for birds, and shade for people, it must first send its roots down deep into the earth. The mighty oak's strength and substance come from its earthy rootedness, for the depth reached by its massive but unseen roots exceeds even the height attained by its towering branches. On the other hand, the palm, which loves the bright and sunny places and may even ascend to great heights, has roots that are shallow and weak; thus, the palm is the first to fall when the ill wind of the hurricane approaches. A tree whose roots do not reach down deep is easily destroyed.

Those of us who would grow toward maturity and wholeness must go down before we can grow up. Like a mighty oak tree, we must be firmly rooted in earthy, ashen soil. Our psychological, emotional, and (especially) spiritual growth is nurtured by the descent into the ashes of pain, brokenness, and human limitation. Without the initiating descent, there may be no spiritual maturity nor depth of character.

On the other hand, those who never descend into the ash pile of life are doomed to emotional shallowness and spiritual immaturity. Like the sun-loving palm whose roots do not reach deep into earthy ashen soil, they lack depth and substance; thus, they are poorly equipped to withstand life's ill winds. In their youth-like arrogance and naiveté, they lack the hard-won wisdom of those whose faces have been smeared with ashes. Like Peter Pan, they remain youths who never grow up: their faces shine and their hair is golden, but their gold is counterfeit, merely the fool's gold of the inexperienced, the untried, and the naive. Though bright-eyed, these eternal youths live in a clouded realm of delusion and denial in which the troubles of humanity are merely rumors or interesting topics of debate in late afternoon gatherings by the pool at the club. Like the inexperienced son of the king in Robert Bly's *Iron John*, they know much about gold, but nothing about poverty. Yet, paradoxically, they are doomed to psychological, emotional, and spiritual impoverishment.

Therefore, the descent into ashes marks the beginning of a difficult transformation from relative superficiality, shallowness, and immaturity to psychological, emotional, and spiritual depth, maturity, and wholeness. Bringing more than just a time of brokenness, sorrow, and hardship, the descent into ashes initiates a period of profound change, growth, and healing for those who endure the crucible of pain and suffering.

To those who knew the taste of ashes, the apostle Peter wrote powerful words of comfort:

> In this you greatly rejoice, though now for a little while you may have had to suffer grief in all kinds of trials. These have come so that your faith—of greater worth than gold, which perishes even though refined by fire—may be proved genuine and may result in praise, glory and honor when Jesus Christ is revealed.
>
> (1 Pet. 1:6–7)

A Caveat

In regard to the journey of spirituality, I would be remiss if I did not warn the reader that merely descending into the ashes of life does not automatically result in a profound spiritual transformation. To be sure, there are those who experience the ash pile of life only to emerge bitter, disillusioned, and cynical as a result of their pain and suffering. If positive psychological, emotional, and (especially) spiritual transformation is to occur, the decent into ashes must be followed by specific spiritual steps.

For help in understanding this vital point, we may look for guidance to the spiritual program known as the Twelve Steps. Those who have practiced the Twelve Steps know the descent into ashes as Step One. With this step, they admit that they are powerless, that they have lost control of their lives. The admission of powerlessness, however, is only the beginning of the profound transformation that may result from the practice of the spiritual principles embodied in the Twelve Steps. Following Step One, Twelve Steppers learn to believe in a power greater than themselves. Next, they are invited to surrender their wills and their lives to God (as they understand him).

In like manner, the descent into ashes is only the beginning of the journey of spirituality. For spiritual transformation to occur, the descent must be followed by faith in the transforming power of God; we must believe that God can, in fact, turn our ashes into gold. We may take heart from the words of the apostle Paul, who assures us that "in all things God works for the good of those who love him" (Rom. 8:28). Moreover, as the Twelve Steps teach, we must surrender our wills and our lives to the divine will. While we will have much more to say about faith and surrender in the pages to follow, suffice it to say for now that we must become willing clay in the hands of the master potter (Isa. 64:8).

CONTEMPORARY ILLUSTRATIONS

Thus far, we have learned that the theme of descent and transformation is repeated not only in fairy tales and folklore, but also in biblical stories. In addition to these sources, contemporary illustrations can deepen our understanding of the universal drama of descent, transformation, and ultimate redemption. Let us examine the lives of Bill Wilson and Charles

Colson, two twentieth-century figures who experienced the descent into ashes in dramatic fashion.

Bill Wilson

Bill Wilson's deep descent into chronic alcoholism caused him to lose everything he thought made him who he was. Although he was once a successful New York stockbroker, as a result of his chronic drinking, Wilson experienced financial ruin, as well as psychological, emotional, and spiritual collapse.

During one of Wilson's many alcohol-related hospitalizations, a former drunk named Ebby, who had maintained sobriety as a result of practicing certain spiritual principles, visited him. Wilson was not quite ready at that first visit to pay attention to spiritual matters, but during a subsequent hospitalization, Ebby visited him again and explained once more the principles that had empowered him to remain sober. After Ebby's second visit, Wilson had an intense spiritual experience which he later described as follows:

> Suddenly the room lit up with a great white light. I was caught up into an ecstasy which there are no words to describe. It seemed to me, in my mind's eye, that I was on a mountain and that a wind not of air but of spirit was blowing. And then it burst upon me that I was a free man. . . . All about me and through me there was a wonderful feeling of Presence. . . . A great peace stole over me and I thought, "No matter how wrong things seem to be, they still are right. Things are all right with God and his world."[4]

After reading William James' *Varieties of Religious Experience,* Wilson learned that intense spiritual experiences such as his "nearly all had the common denominators of pain, suffering and calamity. Complete hopelessness and deflation at depth were almost required to make the recipient ready."[5] Wilson was intimately familiar with "deflation at depth"—what we describe in the present book as the descent into ashes.

After his experience that day in the hospital, Wilson learned to maintain sobriety by sharing his story with other alcoholics. In conjunction with an alcoholic doctor from Ohio, he began a support group for those who wished to recover from alcoholism. Eventually, Wilson authored the Twelve Steps, a program of spiritual principles designed to effectively aid alcoholics in the maintenance of healthy sobriety.

The support group for alcoholics co-founded by "Bill W." is, of course, Alcoholics Anonymous. From its modest beginnings, A.A. has spread throughout the world and is now a readily accessible program of support for those who seek help in overcoming problems related to alcohol abuse. In addition, numerous other support groups have developed that employ, in modified form, the original Twelve Steps of Alcoholics Anonymous (e.g., Overeaters Anonymous, Gamblers Anonymous, Narcotics Anonymous, Relationships Anonymous, Sex and Love Addicts Anonymous, Al-Anon and Alateen). Today, millions of people worldwide practice the spiritual principles embodied in the steps conceived by Bill Wilson, the former drunk now considered one of the greatest social architects of the Twentieth Century. Truly, God turned his ashes into gold.

Charles Colson

Charles Colson is another outstanding example of how God turns ashes into gold. Colson is founder and president of Prison Fellowship, a Christian ministry that brings to those in prison the message of love taught by Jesus of Nazareth, and also seeks to improve conditions in prisons throughout the world. Colson is the author of numerous books, including *Loving God, Kingdoms in Conflict,* and *How Now Shall We Live?*

Colson has written extensively about his imprisonment that was associated with the Watergate scandal of the early 1970s. As a high-ranking official in the Nixon administration, Colson served as a special counsel to the president. He held a position of power and prestige. His office was inside the White House and the president of the United States called him by his first name. Colson had risen to the top; the American dream had come true for him. But then came the fateful Watergate scandal that led to the collapse of the Nixon administration. Colson and others were sentenced to prison.

Charles Colson's descent into ashes was a deep one: from a powerful office in the White House to a prison cell. In this state of powerlessness, Colson came to know a power greater than himself: while in prison, Charles Colson came to know the Lord Jesus Christ.

Colson has commented in his writings about the ironic twist his life has taken. He wrote most cogently about the thoughts he had one day in particular as he awaited his turn to speak at a prison chapel service:

> As I sat on the platform, waiting my turn at the pulpit, my mind began to drift back in time . . . to scholarships and honors earned, cases argued and won, great decisions made from lofty government offices. My life had been the perfect success story, the American dream fulfilled. But all at once I realized it was *not* my success God had used to enable me to help those in this prison, or in hundreds of others just like it. My life of success was not what made this morning so glorious—all my achievements meant nothing in God's economy. No, the real legacy of my life was my biggest failure—that I was an ex-convict. My greatest humiliation—being sent to prison—was the beginning of God's greatest use of my life. He chose the one experience in which I could not glory for his glory.

Confronted with this staggering truth, I discovered in those few moments in the prison chapel that my world was turned upside down. I understood with a jolt that I had been looking at life backward. But now I could see: only when I lost everything I thought made Chuck Colson a great guy had I found the true self God intended me to be and the true purpose of my life.[6]

In prison, in defeat and humiliation, in total powerlessness, Charles Colson's life was transformed. Since that time, through both Prison Fellowship and his numerous books, Colson has helped spread throughout the world the healing message of love taught by Jesus of Nazareth. Also, as a ministry to both soul and body, Prison Fellowship has brought about improvements in the living conditions of those in prison.

IN SUMMARY

Whether found in the lives of contemporary figures such as Bill Wilson and Charles Colson; in fables, fairy tales and folklore; or in the sacred writings of the Holy Bible—the story is always the same: the descent into ashes, that painful plunge into sorrow and suffering that can be taken by many routes, may be a new beginning wherein our lives are transformed by God, the master alchemist who turns our ashes into gold.

CHAPTER 2

Down in Egypt

The way down is the way up.

—Ken Gilburth

L et us now begin a careful examination of an Old Testament story that vividly portrays the universal theme of
descent into ashes followed by a period of trial and transformation. Beginning in the book of Exodus, this story recounts
the Israelites' enslavement in Egypt, their "exodus" from captivity, and their wandering in the wilderness of the Sinai Peninsula.

Before we continue, however, we must examine some of the
controversy that surrounds the ancient biblical stories, especially
those recorded in the Old Testament. Many insist that these
stories are literally true; others argue that these ancient tales are
merely the embellished folklore of an obscure band of Semites
in the ancient Middle East. Invariably, the arguments that
surround the ancient biblical narratives are couched in black-
and-white language: the stories are viewed as either literal,
historical events or as mere fictional allegories. To take one position to the exclusion of the other, however, is to miss a vital
aspect of these stories. Those who view them simply as literal,

historical events may fail to appreciate the depth of their relevance to the modern reader. Likewise, those who discount them as mere fables or allegories fail to understand that the all-ruling God who impacted the lives of the people in these stories is still intensely active in human affairs.

Morton Kelsey, a priest and pastoral counselor, argues that these stories are both historically and metaphorically true.[1] Precisely because they represent universal human truths, God caused these stories to unfold in the drama of human history. These historical events transpired under divine guidance and were recorded by divine inspiration in the Holy Scriptures because they are the stories of us all. As such, they merit careful study and reflection.

INTO THE ASHES OF SLAVERY

The Exodus story is a drama of descent, powerlessness, testing, and transformation. To fully understand the nature of the events that occur in the story, however, we must go back many years earlier to the time of Joseph, the favorite of the twelve sons of the patriarch Jacob.

After being thrown into a dry well by his jealous older brothers, Joseph was sold into slavery and taken to Egypt, where he endured many years of hardship. Joseph's time in the ash pile of suffering and sorrow included both slavery and imprisonment. Because of his divinely gifted ability to interpret dreams, however, he eventually found favor with Pharaoh, the king of Egypt. Joseph was appointed to a position of great authority: he became prime minister of what was then the greatest empire on earth.

Because of Joseph's esteemed position in Egypt, his relatives, who had come to Egypt because of famine in their land, were granted a favorable status in the fertile land of the Nile. During Joseph's tenure as prime minister, and for many years thereafter, his kinsmen, the people of Israel (the Hebrews), enjoyed a politically advantageous position. They prospered both economically and socially, for as the scriptures tell us, they "were fruitful and multiplied greatly and became exceedingly numerous, so that the land was filled with them" (Ex. 1:7). They enjoyed the prosperity that comes to those who find themselves in favorable circumstances.

Ironically, however, their prosperity led them to trouble. A high-level political transition occurred, an event over which the Israelites had no control: "Then a new king, who did not know about Joseph, came to power in Egypt" (Ex. 1:8). The new king was not a member of the "old boy" network; he did not know Joseph. As a result, the Israelites held no special favor in his eyes. In fact, he was alarmed by the sheer number of them; he feared they might join the enemies of Egypt and fight against him. Therefore, the new king enslaved the people and "put slave masters over them to oppress them with forced labor" (Ex. 1:11). Thus, the Israelites fell from the esteemed position of friends of the king to the lowly position of slaves. They were treated ruthlessly by the Egyptians and their lives were made "bitter with hard labor in brick and mortar and with all kinds of work in the fields" (Ex. 1:14a). They had lost control of their lives.

Nevertheless, although the Israelites did not know it, God was already at work among them. Even in the midst of their suffering, God was preparing the way by which he would take them from bondage to freedom. Quietly, without herald or fanfare, a child was born among the Hebrew slaves whom God would later use as their deliverer. The child was Moses.

Because Pharaoh had ordered the death of all male Hebrew babies, Moses' mother, under the watchful eye of God, placed the infant boy in a basket and set him afloat on the Nile River. The baby Moses was found floating among the bulrushes by the daughter of Pharaoh, who took him to the palace and raised him as her own son and a prince of Egypt (Ex. 2:1–10).

When he became a man, Moses "went out to where his own people were and watched them at their hard labor" (Ex. 2:11a). When he saw a guard beating a Hebrew slave, Moses killed the Egyptian soldier and hid the body in the sand. Because his deed was witnessed by others, the young prince—now a murderer—fled Egypt as a fugitive. Thereafter, Moses lived many years as a poor shepherd in the dry and desolate land of Midian in the Sinai wilderness (Ex. 2:11b–15). Thus, as part of his preparation for the great task to which God had called him, Moses descended into ashes. He fell from a position in the royal court of what was then the world's greatest empire to the lowly status of a poor sheepherder in a backwater part of the world.

The Cry of the Broken and the Powerless

During the long period of time while Moses was away, the Israelites groaned under the oppressive yoke of slavery, and they cried out toward heaven (Ex. 2:23).

Like the Hebrews, those of us who are broken and powerless cry out to God. Yet, so often, it seems he does not hear our pleas for help. Perhaps we are suffering through a painful divorce, or we are struggling desperately to break free of an addiction. Perhaps we have lost our jobs, and in the resulting bondage of financial ruin, we fear we may lose our homes. We pray to God for relief from the many difficulties that life brings us, but God seems distant and uncaring, as if he is unconcerned with our pain. We hear the impassioned preacher on Sunday morning television say, "Just pray harder brothers and sisters and all will be well." So we pray harder—and harder. Still the divine answer does not come. We feel as though God has packed his bags, abandoned us, and moved to another universe. For those drowning in sorrow, the distance between the bottom of the well of desperation and the lofty heights of the throne of heaven seems unbridgeable.

Those of us who are honest with ourselves sometimes doubt if God is really concerned for us personally. At times, his silence even causes us to wonder if he exists. Because we dare not share our doubts with others for fear that we will be ostracized from our spiritual communities or, at least, pilloried with guilt, many suffer alone—in silence.

The Exodus story, however, teaches that God does hear our prayers and is concerned about our plight, just as he heard the Israelites cry out to heaven under the oppressive yoke of slavery and was concerned about them (Ex. 2:24–25). Nevertheless, his answer is often long in coming, for God responds according to his timetable, not ours. The enslaved Israelites cried out to God for forty years, a recurring scriptural number that represents a lengthy period of trial and testing. Like the Hebrews, God often allows us to endure trials and difficulties for what may seem a very long period of time before he finally delivers us from bondage.

At the divinely appointed time, God called Moses to Mount Horeb and spoke to him from the burning bush. According to the scriptures:

> The LORD said, "I have indeed seen the misery of my people in Egypt. I have heard them crying out because of their slave drivers, and I am concerned about their suffering. So I have come down to rescue them from the hand of the Egyptians and to bring them up out of that land into a good and spacious land, a land flowing with milk and honey . . . So now, go. I am sending you to Pharaoh to bring my people the Israelites out of Egypt."
>
> (Ex. 3:7–10)

God does indeed hear the groans and plaintive cries that come from deep within the pit of pain and suffering. When the burden upon the Israelites became virtually unbearable, when it appeared there was no room left for even a glimmer of hope,

God sent Moses to lead the people out of bondage. The descent into ashes set the stage for redemption, for God longed for his people to cry out to him from the ash pile of sorrow, powerlessness, and defeat. Then upon their coming deliverance, they would know who brought them out of the land of suffering, from the mud pits of slavery to the Promised Land flowing with milk and honey.

DARKEST BEFORE DAWN

When Moses, assisted by Aaron, appeared at court to confront Pharaoh, things did not immediately improve for the Israelites. In fact, after Moses' initial meeting with the Egyptian king, matters took a distinctly downward turn. Moses had asked the king to allow the people to go into the desert to celebrate a festival in honor of God. Yet not only did the king refuse the request, but "[t]hat same day Pharaoh gave this order to the slave drivers and foremen in charge of the people: 'You are no longer to supply the people with straw for making bricks; let them go and gather their own straw. But require them to make the same number of bricks as before'" (Ex. 5:6–8). On the eve of their deliverance, the people's bondage grew measurably heavier. Not only did they have to make the same number of bricks; now they had to gather the straw as well. For the Israelites the old adage proved true: "It is darkest just before the dawn."

A POWER GREATER THAN THEMSELVES

Because of the increased burden the Egyptian king placed upon the Israelites, their leaders blamed Moses for their predicament. They said, "May the LORD look upon you [Moses] and judge you! You have made us a stench to Pharaoh and his officials and have put a sword in their hand to kill us" (Ex. 5:21). Earlier, when they learned that God was concerned about their plight and suffering, they worshiped (Ex. 4:31). Now that matters had taken a turn for the worse, they blamed Moses for their troubles. No doubt, much of their animosity was directed toward heaven as well.

Many of us who have been down into ashes have vacillated in our feelings toward God. At one moment we beg God for help; the next moment we complain because we do not approve of his methods. All too often we think we know better than God. We want to tell God how we should be lifted out of the pit. Not only do we demand he let down a rope, but we tell him what kind of rope to use.

Moreover, when we first land hard in the ash heap of pain, brokenness, and human limitation, we cling to the lingering misconception that we can save ourselves. Deluded by an illusion of self-sufficiency, we insist that we can free ourselves from bondage. Emboldened by our innate sense of omnipotence, we connive, collude, and conceive all manner of plans to take charge once again, to regain control of our lives. Most of us do not easily surrender the desire to act as captain of our own fate and run our own show.

In the Exodus story, God left the people in the ash pile long enough to fully realize they could not save themselves. He patiently allowed events to unfold so they would learn that only divine intervention could save them. For the Hebrews, the lingering remnants of the illusion of self-sufficiency slowly evaporated in the sweltering heat of the Egyptian sun.

God's purposes have not changed in the thousands of years since the Exodus story. He still deeply desires that the broken and powerless know the identity of the true Higher Power. Those who feel crushed by divorce, illness, addiction, loss of a job, or any of the myriad means by which life takes us down into ashes, need divine assistance in order to return to health and wholeness. After we have spent a lengthy period of time in the ash pile, our illusions of self-sufficiency slowly melt away, and we finally realize that only a power greater than ourselves can restore us.

DISCOURAGEMENT, DOUBT, AND DISAPPOINTMENT

As we return to the plight of the Israelites in Egypt, we might expect the story to take a decidedly upward turn, that the people would finally recognize their need for divine intervention and would take heart in God's reassurance of forthcoming deliverance. If the Exodus story were a tidy allegory or merely a child's fairy tale, we would expect Moses to return triumphantly to the people with God's message, there to receive a great ovation of cheers and praises, followed by a solemn, consensual commitment to obey the commands of God. Yet the Exodus story is not merely a fable designed to teach the value of patience or the ultimate redemption of the virtuous; rather, it is the story of real people, in a real place, in a real time. Thus, like all portrayals of human nature painted with the brush of realism, it is not neat, clean, and tidy. The Scriptures tell us that when Moses reported to the people all the things God had told him, "they did not listen to him because of their discouragement and cruel bondage" (Ex. 6:9). They did not receive Moses' report with cheery optimism nor the Pollyannaish naiveté of those who have never experienced the ashes of life. Instead, they were discouraged because of the tremendous weight of their oppression. For a long, hard time their constant companions had been hopelessness, despair, and a deeply felt sense of disappointment with God.

Like the ancient Israelites, many of us find ourselves discouraged because of enslavement. Our modern captivity, however, is usually psychological, emotional, and spiritual; and is felt in varying forms: hopelessness and despair; loneliness; lack of meaning and purpose in life; restlessness; lack of fulfillment, both personal and vocational; and lack of freedom. For many, the pain of captivity is felt as a deep sense of social, environmental, and spiritual alienation. Hidden behind socially protective masks and encased in emotional armor, we are distanced from each other. Because of industrialization and the mass migration to the city, many of us have lost our roots and our relationship to the earth. As a result of the materialistic secularization of our society, too many have forfeited a connection to the sacred, becoming islands in a vast ocean with no bridges between them.

On a microcosmic level, much of our modern bondage is rooted in dysfunctional families and stems from painful and shaming childhood and teen-years experiences. The resulting dysfunction manifests itself in different ways: Therapists' offices, for example, are frequented by emotionally empty women who engage in one sexual liaison after another to compensate for their fathers' rejection. Stress, burnout, and heart attacks plague many entrepreneurs who feverishly climb an ever-higher ladder of success to compensate for parental labels of incompetent and inadequate. Many of Hollywood's young male sitcom writers stereotypically cast all middle-aged men as fools and buffoons to displace their repressed rage toward the fathers who rejected them. The consequent, rapid rise of the broad based adult-child movement bears testimony to our deeply felt sense of captivity.

Disconnected from each other, from the earth, and from our Creator, we are tormented by a lonely feeling of alienation. Unbelievers peer into the heavens and see nothing but the blackness of the void. For those of us who are believers, the cold silence that can engulf our unanswered questions and prayers is sometimes deafening. Our severe alienation, coupled with a felt sense of meaninglessness, compels many among us to engage in various behaviors whose goal is to provide an illusion of control that fosters a fleeting sense of happiness and well-being in this world of suffering. So we use drugs, alcohol, food, or one another to medicate the pain of alienation, meaninglessness, and despair.

What is the solution to our modern predicament? Is there a way out of our psychological, emotional, and spiritual captivity? The Exodus story teaches that there is indeed a way to freedom, a way that we will examine in detail in the pages to come.

THE WAY DOWN IS THE WAY UP

For 430 years, the people of Israel were *down* in Egypt. Though at one time, they had enjoyed a favorable, prosperous relationship with the powers of the land, political events completely beyond their control ushered in their descent into humiliating, powerless enslavement. Their final years in Egypt were marked by cruel bondage, hardship, misery, and suffering. Their last weeks and months of captivity were marked by oscillating cycles of hope followed by disappointment, as a fickle king promised freedom one day only to snatch it away the next. Finally, after a series of horrendous plagues devastated the Egyptian empire (Ex. chapters 7–12), they were set free from slavery. Under the leadership of Moses, the Hebrews, numbering perhaps more than two million people (*cf.* Ex. 12:37–38), then began their exodus (*exit*) from Egypt, bound for the place promised for generations as their inheritance: the land flowing with milk and honey.

The extraordinary events experienced by the people of Israel were divinely orchestrated. God's plan was unfolding even as they descended into slavery. The Israelites were like clay in the hands of the master potter. God was molding and shaping them into vessels suitable for a divine purpose: they were to establish the first monotheistic nation in an ancient world replete with pagan polytheism; they were to receive and promulgate the codified commandments, God's divine law in written form; they were to build the most magnificent building of the ancient world, the great temple of God in Jerusalem; and, most importantly, the Hebrew slaves were to embody the cultural matrix from which the promised Messiah would come. In order for this band of Semitic nomads to grow into their high calling, they had to undergo a time of testing and transformation, of which the descent into ashes was only the beginning. For the Israelites, the road that would eventually lead to the Promised Land passed first through the mud pits of slavery and back-breaking bondage.

Like the Hebrew slaves in Egypt, those who have experienced the deep descent into ashes and have hit bottom may feel as though life is over, that they have reached the end of a long, hard road. Those suffering through a heartbreaking divorce commonly see no hope for the future as their dreams of a happy home and family lie shattered at their feet. Persons whose careers have ended in ashes because of economic or political events beyond their control often see themselves doomed to the slavery of low-paying, monotonous, meaningless jobs taken solely to make ends meet. Because the ashes of their former lives are all that remain, those who have lost spouses, jobs, homes, and friends because of a long captivity to addiction feel that life has left them behind. Those who endure debilitating illnesses find neither meaning in their suffering nor hope for healing. Yet strangely enough, as was the case for the Israelites, the descent into ashes marks the beginning of a new journey rather than only the painful end of an old one. According to my friend and fellow therapist Ken Gilburth, "The way down is the way up." This terse phrase tells us that the descent into ashes is actually the beginning of the road to discovery, recovery, and wholeness. Psychologically, emotionally, and spiritually, the high road to maturity and wholeness leads first through the ashen lowlands of powerlessness and defeat.

LOOKING AHEAD

As we have seen, the Exodus is a story of a fall, of going *down* into Egypt. It is a saga of those who have experienced powerlessness and the bitter disappointment of shattered dreams, a tale of those who have traveled the path poet Robert Bly called "the road of ashes, descent, and grief."[2]

As stated earlier, the Exodus story is universal; that is, the saga of the Israelites' journey from Egypt to the land of milk and honey represents the experience of all people in all places throughout time. In other words, *the Exodus story is your story and my story.* To be sure, at some point in our lives, we all will be called to journey from Egypt to the promised land.

Moreover, since the Exodus story is a universal experience, a human drama that rings true for people everywhere throughout the ages, we should expect to find in this great saga elements and events that, either symbolically or literally, dramatize the unfolding events in our own lives. Furthermore, by careful study of this historical, epic account of release from bondage and powerlessness, we may discover not only a metaphorical representation of past and present events of our own lives, but future ones as well. By careful review of the events, expectations, and emotions that weave this story into a meaningful whole, we may garner instructive insight into the events, expectations, and emotions that will characterize our own journeys from pain and brokenness to wholeness, peace, and contentment. In other words, as we come to understand that we have been where they were, we may also gain the invaluable insight that we are going where they went! Thus, we do well to continue the careful study of the universally human events that surrounded the lives of those who traveled the road of ashes, descent, and grief before us.

CHAPTER 3

Escape to Freedom

The just shall live by faith, not by sight.

—The apostle Paul

Before we look at the Exodus story in greater detail, we must firmly fix an essential point in our minds: the journey from Egypt to the promised land, from bondage and brokenness to freedom and wholeness, is far more than a period of psychological and emotional change and growth. At its elemental or basic level, the journey from ashes into gold is a *spiritual* journey, a time of testing, trial, and transformation during which our old (and often inaccurate) ideas of God, as well as our deeply ingrained convictions about the nature of the spiritual life, are profoundly altered. As others who have made this arduous journey can attest, those who emerge on the other side of this difficult time of spiritual transformation are radically changed in their relationships to God, to others, and to themselves.

THE NATURE OF THE JOURNEY

What is the nature of the spiritual journey? At least in a general way, what can we expect to encounter along the path that leads from brokenness to wholeness, from ashes into gold?

We gain deeper insight into the nature of the spiritual journey by traveling to the opposite side of the world—to Nara, a suburb of Tokyo, Japan. The small city of Nara is the site of a great temple, a magnificent religious shrine known as the Temple of Life. The temple sits peacefully in the middle of a beautiful, fragrant garden. Leading to it is a long, winding path guarded on either side by two ugly, fierce dragons. The first dragon is called Fear; the second, Desire. The message so dramatically portrayed by the layout of the temple and its surrounding grounds is profoundly symbolic, for it is a metaphorical representation of the journey of spirituality: to get to the Temple of Life in the middle of the garden, we must first travel the long winding path guarded by Fear and Desire.[1]

All who undertake the journey of spirituality must confront the dragons called Fear and Desire. In the pages to come, we will examine the various manifestations of these two protean beasts.

But first, we must return to the ancient story of the Exodus, where the Israelites are soon to encounter the first of the beasts that guard the winding path that leads to the Promised Land.

THE DRAGON OF FEAR

When the people of Israel were enslaved in Egypt, they cried out to God, for they knew they were powerless to save themselves. Their admission of powerlessness, however, was only the beginning of their journey. Soon after their exodus from Egypt, the Israelites learned that they must take another vital step on the road to the land of promise.

Only a few weeks after leaving Goshen, their former home in the land of the Nile, the Israelites camped by the Red Sea.

There on the windy shore at the edge of Egypt, at the threshold of freedom, they encountered the frightening beast named Fear.

To their horror, the Israelites discovered they were not yet rid of the fickle king at whose fingers they had bobbed like puppets. Soon after the Israelites had begun their exodus from Egypt, Pharaoh, the Egyptian king, regretted having set free the slaves so economically vital to his country. Therefore, "he had his chariot made ready and took his army with him. He took six hundred of the best chariots, along with all the other chariots of Egypt, with officers over all of them" and pursued the Israelites into the desert (Ex. 14:6–8). Without warning, the Hebrew people were suddenly panic-stricken at the approaching sound of thundering hooves, creaking chariot wheels, and clanging armor. When they saw Pharaoh with his army and hundreds of chariots advancing in the distance, they were terrified. They believed they were about to be slaughtered like sheep in the desert.

At first the people cried out to God for help, but in fear, they quickly turned on Moses. They said:

> Was it because there were no graves in Egypt that you brought us to the desert to die? What have you done to us by bringing us out of Egypt? Didn't we say to you in Egypt, "Leave us alone; let us serve the Egyptians"? It would have been better for us to serve the Egyptians than to die in the desert!
>
> (Ex. 14:11–12)

At the first sign of trouble, the Israelites cried out in regret that they had dared to risk the perils of the escape to freedom. Though their daily routine had been only bitter suffering, backbreaking labor, and unending misery, they wanted to give up, saying it would have been better to remain slaves in Egypt than to face the dangers that suddenly lay before them. The Israelites quickly fell into the woeful thinking that fosters dependency and bondage: "It would have been better" to remain stuck in slavery, to endure misery than to risk the dangers of the journey to freedom. Those faithless words simply mean that, in the face of fear and danger, the misery of the status quo seems preferable to the terrifying risks of change.

FAMILIAR MISERY AND THE FEAR OF CHANGE

As the Israelites cowered beneath the roaring dragon of fear, they quickly learned that the escape to freedom is not easy. The journey from the land of bondage is difficult, for slavery or dependency of any kind is like a devouring pit that sucks human beings into it. All who embark on the path to freedom face great hardship. Whether we are enslaved to addiction, compulsive behavior, an abusive spouse, an unhealthy relationship, or a job we hate, the climb out is long, painful, and tiring. We may easily lose strength and slide back in.

Because the escape to freedom is fraught with perils that are unknown and unfamiliar, many remain in slavery. Many prefer the familiar misery of slavery and drudgery to the unfamiliar risks inherent in the escape to freedom. Like the terrified Israelites who said it would have been better to remain in Egypt, many fear the uncertain, frightening territory of change.

In our society, for example, many people remain trapped in unfulfilling jobs they hate because they are afraid of the frightening, uncertain consequences of change. Harold, a forty-year-old husband and father of three teenagers, came to counseling because of depression. As the first session began, Harold told me that he had worked most of his adult life as an insurance claims adjuster. As the hour progressed, I learned that Harold was by nature an introverted, quiet man; thus, he was particularly unsuited for a job that routinely involved unpleasant confrontations with customers dissatisfied with the insurance reimbursements offered by his company. Harold revealed that, more days than not, he dreaded going to work. As could be expected, Harold's unhappiness at work adversely affected his family life. Most evenings, Harold returned home from work irritable and frustrated because of distasteful altercations with one or more claimees. He often took his frustration out on his wife Betty, a habit that had caused her to emotionally withdraw to a safe distance. His three teenage children typically took to their rooms when Harold came home in hopes of avoiding a father whose moods were more like those of a grizzly bear than a loving dad. Certainly, no one in Harold's family would object to a career move on his part.

Like many others, Harold dreamed of starting a little family-operated business "some day." Because he loved to create lovely gardens with plants, shrubs, and flowers—and often did so for free in the yards of his appreciative friends and neighbors—he had long wanted to open a small landscaping business. Clearly he had the talent, and his willing wife and three teenagers could easily provide him all the help he needed. Furthermore, Harold and Betty had several thousand dollars in their savings account, money that Harold had always insisted be put aside for a rainy day. To be sure, the money was more than enough to start a small business out of their home and carry them through the first difficult months of getting established.

Sadly, however, Harold refused to leave his unfulfilling job as a claims adjuster because he was afraid to surrender the security of a weekly paycheck. His fear, represented by an endless list of questions, kept him stuck in a career that, for him, was pure slavery. What about college for the children? What if they had to have a new car? How dare he forfeit the excellent health insurance provided by his company? Where would he find customers? What if no one was willing to pay for his services as a landscaper? To be sure, Harold's fear had blinded him to the real opportunities that lay before him.

Unhappily, because of his fear, Harold refused to enter the unknown territory of change and growth that stood between him and the career of his dreams waiting on the other side. After only two sessions, Harold terminated counseling, saying that he had decided to see a psychiatrist whom he felt sure would provide him a prescription to chemically solve his problem with depression. He failed to see that his depression was a symptom of his bondage. Like so many of us today, Harold was a slave, a man who had sacrificed his life to a job he hated in exchange for the security of a weekly paycheck.

Like those enslaved to jobs they hate, many held captive by addiction fear change. Those trapped in chemical dependency, for example, fear the prospects of living without the crutch of their drug of choice. Bill, a thirty-seven-year-old alcoholic who recently came to me for counseling, was terrified by the prospect of sobriety. Near the beginning of one of our sessions he said, "I get so bored sitting around the apartment after work. I don't have anything to do if I don't drink." I encouraged him to develop a hobby, take dancing lessons, enroll in night school, start working out at a local gym, or attend A.A. meetings each evening, anything to occupy his time and keep his mind off drinking. He objected to all these suggestions, saying that he was too shy to try anything new without a couple of beers to help him feel better about himself. He also said that he didn't like A.A. meetings; he was tired of hearing about alcoholism. For Bill, sobriety was truly unfamiliar territory. Life without the crutch of alcohol was strange and frightening. Although he had lost his marriage and had been fired from two jobs because of his drinking, he preferred the familiar misery of active addiction to the unfamiliar territory of sobriety. After four weeks, he did not return to counseling.

Like chemical dependents, those trapped in abusive relationships often return to familiar slavery rather than risk the perils of the escape to freedom. Consider, for example, a frequent visitor to the therapist's office: the woman who is involved with an abusive man. She comes to therapy with a familiar tale of beatings, verbal abuse, and sexual infidelity on the part of her partner, behavior often related to his abuse of alcohol. Frustrated by her many failed attempts to change her partner, the distraught woman hopes to find in counseling a quick fix to her problems. She believes that if the therapist will tell her the magic secret, she will finally be able to change her partner's behavior and her life will suddenly and dramatically improve. As is typical in such cases, she believes that if she can change him, all will be well.

When I counsel a client who is involved in an abusive relationship, I ask her an important question: "Do you want things to change, or do you want them to stay the same?" Invariably she will reply: "Oh, I want things to change; I can't stand it this way anymore." (That, of course, is the reason she came to therapy in the first place.) "In that case," I say, "one of two things will happen: either the relationship will get better, or it will get worse." (In fact, the relationship generally gets worse before it gets better, *if* it gets better). She typically responds that she is willing to chance the outcome. "Anything is better than this," she says. Then we spend the remainder of the first session dispelling the notion that she can change him, since the only person she can change is herself. Thus the first session ends with the client pumped up and ready to take on every dragon in the forest—until she goes home and encounters the beast she is living with!

One of the dynamics of family systems is that when one person in the system attempts to change, the others in the system often resist the change. In other words, they try to maintain the comfortable, familiar status quo. Healthy change, however, fosters growth. Moreover, if one is to grow, those who surround her must give her elbowroom. Nevertheless, people in familiar, comfortable positions do not like elbows stuck in their ribs. Indeed, they resent those who are stretching out their arms, seeking room to grow. Therefore, as the client, determined to change, leaves her counseling session and returns home, her efforts are neither applauded nor approved; rather, they are resisted.

In relationships that involve abuse, the abuser is generally comfortable in his position; he is pleased with his dictatorial reign and does not want the relationship to change. When his partner begins to behave in new, unfamiliar ways, he becomes frightened (a fact he is not likely to admit), and he masks his fear with anger. Because he feels intimidated and threatened by her new behavior, he threatens his partner and attempts to intimidate her with verbal and, sometimes, physical abuse. Because he does not like the changes she is making, he exerts great effort to keep things the same: he berates her for her "selfishness" and lack of concern for the relationship; he vows to "straighten out that counselor" she has been seeing; he accuses her of infidelity and threatens divorce.

Therefore, both partners are confronted with the possibility of change, and both are afraid. The abusive spouse, frightened by new, unfamiliar behavior, may make good his threats and abandon his partner, for running away seems easier than wrestling with change. Since women in abusive relationships are often unemployed or underemployed and lack the skills to secure a well-paid job, she may risk the loss of financial security if divorced. When children are involved, the stakes are exponentially higher. As she begins to think about her future, one that may find her divorced and alone, a thousand questions come to mind, ones that usually begin with the terrifying phrase that is the bane of all who would change: What if? What if I can't find a job? What if I can't pay the rent? What if he leaves the state and refuses to pay child support? What if I can't afford day care? What if we lose our medical insurance? What if I have to live alone the rest of my life? The questions and the unknown possibilities of the realm of change are both endless and terrifying.

Thus, the cards are laid on the table, and it's time to gamble. The abused spouse must decide if she is willing to accept the risks of change. If she chooses to escape the abusive relationship, she must be willing to pay the price, and—make no mistake—the cost of freedom is high. Sadly, often after only three or four weeks of counseling, the frightened woman gives up the fight and returns to her enslavement to an abusive spouse. Once again, the familiar misery of slavery seems preferable to the unfamiliar territory of change.

As a therapist, I have felt frustrated and saddened to watch a client return to an abusive relationship rather than risk the perils of the journey from bondage. Because even slavery offers a measure of predictability and security, too often we prefer its familiar misery to the uncertainty of a new way of life. Thus, time and again, we remain trapped because we fear the unknown territory of change. Why else would so many return to slavery rather than risk the inherent uncertainties of the escape to freedom?

UNCHARTED TERRITORY

Most of us like to have a plan before we set out on a journey. In preparation for driving a great distance, many take a map and sit in a comfortable chair the night before to plan the route that will take us expeditiously to our destinations. To avoid making wrong turns along the way, some mark the exact route with a red pencil or a colored marker. To assure ourselves of a safe and timely arrival, we want precise directions to our destination before we start out.

The territory of change, however, is not only an unfamiliar one, but it is an uncharted one as well. In other words, *there is no map.* When the people of Israel left the slavery of Egypt, they knew they were bound for a land flowing with milk and honey, a land they had only heard of, and one they had little idea how to reach. Like the Hebrews, those of us who embark on the spiritual journey that begins in bondage and brokenness know only that we wish to journey to a place of freedom and wholeness; yet, we have no idea how we will get there. One thing is certain, however. As it was for the people of Israel, so it is for us: to escape the familiar misery of slavery and arrive at the land flowing with milk and honey, we must venture into the unfamiliar, uncharted, and frightening territory of change.

THE SHIELD OF FAITH

Because the territory of change and growth is a dark, fearsome, and uncharted region, many refuse to enter therein, for we are afraid to set out without a map that shows the way to our destination. Frankly, we desire a map that details the exact route to freedom because we want to live by sight rather than by faith. However, the Holy Bible, God's word in written form, directs us toward an opposite approach to life: that is, to live by faith, not by sight (2 Cor. 5:7). "Faith," according to the New Testament Book of Hebrews, "is being sure of what we hope for and certain of what we do not see" (Heb. 11:1). All who risk the dark perils of the unknown, unseen territory of change must venture forth in faith. Since there is no map to the land flowing with milk and honey, we must journey forward even though we cannot see where we are going.

Caught between the waves of the Red Sea in front of them and Pharaoh's army and chariots behind them, the people of Israel were uncertain which way to go next. Because they could see no way out of their dilemma, they feared they were about to die in the desert, the prey of the vengeful Egyptians.

Moses told them, however, "Do not be afraid. Stand firm and you will see the deliverance the LORD will bring you today. . . . The LORD will fight for you; you need only to be still" (Ex. 14:13–14). Then God said to Moses, "Tell the Israelites to move on. Raise your staff and stretch out your hand over the sea to divide the water so that the Israelites can go through the sea on dry ground" (Ex. 14:15b–16). Next, to prevent Pharaoh's chariots from overrunning the Israelites, God assumed the form of a pillar of cloud and stood between them and the Egyptian army (Ex. 14:19–20). Finally, "Moses stretched out his hand over the sea, and all that night the LORD drove the sea back with a strong east wind and turned it into dry land. The waters were divided, and the Israelites went through the sea on dry ground, with a wall of water on their right and on their left" (Ex. 14:21 22).

As we read the scriptural account, we may easily allow the brevity of the narrative to obscure the human drama that must have taken place. If, however, we put ourselves in their place through the use of imagination, perhaps we can appreciate the anxiety and fear felt by the Israelites when Moses signaled with his staff for them to walk between the towering walls of water. Behind them they heard the clanking of swords and armor, the snorting of Egyptian war-horses, and the cursing of hostile soldiers ready to slit their throats. Before them loomed two rising walls of water, held back by an eerie east wind and leaving between them a gap that surely must have seemed the valley of death. Their predicament was terrifying; no doubt, it seemed hopeless as well. They had no easy choice. To turn back meant either death at the hands of the Egyptians or, at best, a return to slavery for the remainder of their lives. To go forward meant the risk of drowning in the sea, for they had no certainty that the towering waters would not crash down and destroy them. To be sure, the terrifying dragon of fear roared loudly there on the shore of the Red Sea.

The frightful bellowing of the beast, however, signals the time to take up the surest defense against the dragon of fear: the shield of faith. Certainly that was the case for the Hebrews, for great faith was required of them as they stood on that windy shore: the kind of faith that results in trusting action; the kind of faith that is required when God commands us to go forward, even when the way is frightening.

Finally, the Hebrews chose the way of the sea. At Moses' command, they passed between the walls of water to safety on the other side. The Egyptians foolishly tried to follow, but were inundated by the collapsing walls of water and drowned (Ex. 14:23–28). Thus ended a long, dark period of slavery and powerlessness for the people of Israel. Because they trusted in God, who was ready, willing, and able to save them, they escaped to freedom and continued their uncharted journey from Egypt toward the land flowing with milk and honey.

No Easier, Softer Way

Like the Israelites of old, all who embark on the path of change and growth will arrive at the shore of the Red Sea. There, at the threshold of freedom, they will encounter the dragon named Fear. The newly divorced will fear loneliness, single-parenting, and financial insecurity. Those who escape the slavery of jobs they hate will fear financial ruin and the uncertainty of living hand-to-mouth. Chemical dependents, struggling through the early days of recovery, will fear the prospects of living without the artificial support of their drug of choice. Compulsive gamblers, who have routinely sought the thrill of a quick fix to their financial problems, will fear the prospect of the long, slow climb out of debt. Workaholics will fear to lower their masks and open themselves to the intimacy in which they are known by more than a corporate title. Relationship addicts will fear loneliness, and people-pleasers will fear dispensability. Like the Greek god Proteus, who had the power to assume any shape or form, the dragon of fear will appear to each of us in the appropriate disguise.

Many who read these words are standing on the shore of the Red Sea. You have heard the awful roar of the dragon of fear who guards the winding path to freedom. You feel frightened, alone, and uncertain, not knowing which way to turn. Your fear is heightened because you cannot see a way out of your painful dilemma. Thus, you think of returning to the familiar misery from which you have so long wanted to be free.

Yet, those who are standing on that lonely, windy shore, at that point of decision to which the journey of change and growth always leads, must take heart in the absolute fact that God will show you the way out of your place of bondage and all-too-familiar misery—if you will only trust him. But as we have seen in the harrowing experiences of the Hebrew people, God may first require you to be still and wait for him to open the way to freedom, and that wait may seem a very long one. Finally, he will make a path and invite you to follow it.

The path God opens may be very different from the one you had in mind, and it will seem more difficult than the easier, softer way you would have chosen for yourself. The terrifying path that God opened through the sea was assuredly not the one the Israelites would have chosen for themselves. Certainly God could have made matters easier for them. He could have sent a fleet of ferries piloted by angels to take them comfortably across the sea, or he could have removed the threat to their lives by instantly destroying the Egyptians. But by so doing, he would have precluded the need for trust on the part of the people. Thus, instead of providing them an easier way, God required them to take a route they would never have considered themselves: he asked them to demonstrate their faith by stepping into the valley of death left in the gap between the towering walls of water. The Israelites were given only two choices: either return to slavery or go forward and risk the perils of the sea. Because the looming specter of death hovered in either direction, there was no easy way out.

Like the Israelites, when you reach your Red Sea, you also will have two choices: either return to slavery and familiar misery or go forward. Both choices are difficult, and there is no easier, softer way. If you are to escape the land of bondage, however, and venture beyond the threshold of freedom into the uncharted wilderness of change and growth, you must first be still and wait at the shore of the Red Sea for God's guidance. After you have received it, you must move forward by taking the step of faith. You must walk between the towering walls of water and trust God to keep you dry.

The case of a thirty-eight-year-old woman I recently counseled illustrates the difficulty of crossing the threshold to freedom. Barbara, a third grade teacher at a local elementary school, had been enslaved in an abusive relationship for sixteen years. Her husband had verbally abused her repeatedly and had physically abused her several times, twice causing her to go to the emergency room for stitches. For years she had passively endured his alcohol abuse and multiple affairs, three of them long term. He had even brought other women into their marriage bed when Barbara was away visiting her mother. Unable to withstand the abuse any longer, she finally left him and sought counseling. During the first session, she told me she was thinking of filing for divorce. I asked her pointedly what was stopping her. She answered with one word: "Fear." Then she explained that she was afraid her teacher's salary would not be enough to support her; she was afraid of what her husband might do to her when he received divorce papers; she was afraid of living alone the rest of her life. (Not ruling out the possibility of reconciliation under completely different terms), I told her that she stood at the shore of the Red Sea, and like the ancient Hebrews, she had two choices: she could go backward, or she could go forward. To go backward meant a return to the slavery of an abusive relationship that was a marriage in name only. To go forward meant that, like the Israelites, she must take up the shield of faith against the dragon of fear and step into the breach formed by the towering walls of water. She prayed about her situation over the following weeks and contemplated life in the unknown wilderness of change and growth, that frightening, unfamiliar territory that lay in the distance, just beyond the threshold to freedom. When she arrived at her eighth session, I immediately noticed a difference in her appearance. Her eyes were no longer red and swollen from crying; instead, they were clear and harbored a look of peace, contentment, and serenity. Sitting in the chair across from me, she seemed less nervous and did not wring her hands as she had in previous sessions. I asked her what had happened to account for the change in her demeanor. She told me that she had decided she would no longer allow herself to be enslaved and abused by her Pharaoh-like husband; therefore, three days earlier she had filed for divorce. She said that through a combination of counseling, prayer, Bible reading, and deep soul searching, she had come to believe that God would be with her through the unknown, perilous days ahead. "In other words," she said with a determined sparkle in her eye, "I have decided to pick up my shield and step into the sea."

> No temptation has seized you except what is common to man. And God is faithful; he will not let you be tempted beyond what you can bear. But when you are tempted, he will also provide a way out so that you can stand up under it.
>
> (1 Cor. 10:13)

CHAPTER 4

Into the Wilderness

Because we easily imagine ourselves in want, we imagine God ready to forsake us.

—George MacDonald[1]

I was young and now I am old, yet I have never seen the righteous forsaken nor their children begging bread.

—King David of Israel

T he miraculous deliverance of the Israelites at the Red Sea teaches us that God will provide a way out of the inevitable difficulties encountered by those who travel the journey of faith. Like the Israelites, our task is to trust in God's leading and follow the path he opens before us.

Once we have embarked on that path, however, we must continue to journey by faith, for our difficulties are not all behind us. Many challenges still lie ahead in the unknown, unfamiliar wilderness of change and growth. Such was the case for the Israelites as they left the Red Sea behind them and entered the wilderness of Sinai.

LONGING FOR EGYPT

Soon after the dramatic events at the Red Sea, God led the Hebrews into the Sinai Peninsula, an arid, sparsely vegetated wilderness that lacked enough wild game and vegetation to feed the vast throng of more than two million people; thus, they soon succumbed to hunger. Because they appeared to be stranded with no provisions for their survival, they began to complain to Moses. They said, "If only we had died by the LORD's hand in Egypt! There we sat around pots of meat and ate all the food we wanted, but you have brought us out into this desert to starve this entire assembly to death" (Ex. 16:3).

As we look back across history to the experience of the Hebrews, we may think that because they witnessed such a vivid display of divine intervention at the Red Sea, they would continue their journey to the Promised Land filled with faith, optimism, and cheerfulness, secure in the knowledge that the God of the heavens was their friend and ally. Such was not the case, however, for as we have already noted, the Exodus story is about real people, frail human beings who complained, doubted, and often wanted to give up. Their journey through the wilderness was not a smooth one; the journey of spirituality never is. To the contrary, it was marked more by peaks and valleys of faith and doubt than by a smooth, steady climb toward spiritual wholeness.

The Israelites had witnessed some of God's greatest miracles. Few times in history has God intervened on behalf of his people in such dramatic fashion. Nevertheless, the memories of both the divinely wrought plagues that ushered in their release from Egypt (Ex. 7–11) and the cataclysmic display of divine power at the Red Sea were not enough to strengthen them against the common problem of hunger. According to the hierarchy of needs described by psychologist Abraham Maslow, the satisfaction of physical needs must precede the satisfaction of all other needs. As any missionary to the famine-stricken regions of Africa can attest, people need physical food before they are ready for spiritual food.

As the Hebrews grew weaker from hunger, they began to think of their former days in Egypt. Note what they said: "In Egypt we had all the food we wanted." Because the heat and deprivation of the Sinai wilderness had distorted their memories, they began to long for a return to the familiar misery of the past, to "the good old days" when they had enough to eat. In the harsh conditions of the wilderness of change and growth, they forgot about the years of backbreaking bondage when they trudged like beasts of burden beneath the heavy loads of bricks they carried for Pharaoh's building projects. They forgot the sting of the taskmaster's whip and the hopelessness and despair they felt as they treaded mud and straw with their bare, callused feet. For the moment, the pain of change and growth seemed worse than the agony of slavery.

Today, those of us who tread the path of change and growth frequently react to adversity as did the Israelites, for the hardships of the journey of faith cloud our memories as well. Because the winding path through the wilderness of change and growth is fraught with difficulties, thoughts of turning back are common. New divorcées, their memories clouded by loneliness and grief, commonly forget the problems of their previous marriages and quickly attach themselves to new partners whose dysfunctions mirror those of their former spouses. Many insecure, dependent women remember the strong, secure arms of the spouse or lover who took care of them, but they forget or minimize the severity of the beatings and abuse they received. Many recovering alcoholics fondly recall the good old days of wine, sex, and song, while forgetting the hangovers, heartaches, broken marriages, and lost jobs. Habitual gamblers often long for the thrill of winning the big bet, even those who sleep in rescue missions instead of the homes they gambled away. And upon receiving their first late payment notice, those who embark on the careers of their dreams forget the emptiness and drudgery of the unfulfilling jobs they left behind. To be sure, there are times in the harsh wilderness of change and growth when even slavery looks good! Like the starving Israelites who hungered for the "pots of meat" of Egypt, we sometimes long for the days when, at least to our selective memories, things seemed easier.

One Day at a Time

God heard the grumbling and complaining of the Israelites. As always, he remained sensitive to the needs of his people. Thus God said to Moses: "I will rain down bread from heaven for you. The people are to go out each day and gather enough for that day" (Ex. 16:4). God also sent quail into the camp so the people would have meat. As God said, "At twilight you will eat meat, and in the morning you will be filled with bread. Then you will know that I am the LORD your God" (Ex. 16:12). That evening, quail flew into the camp by the thousands; the next morning, the bread from heaven covered the ground like dew. Moses instructed the people to gather only as much of the bread, or *manna,* as they needed for that day. If they gathered more, the excess would spoil over night and become unfit to eat (Ex. 16:13–20). Thus, God promised to provide his people exactly what they needed for that day.

With the miracle of the manna from heaven, God established a manner of living that the Hebrews would follow for forty years as they wandered through the Sinai wilderness (Ex. 16:35). Today, that way of living remains an integral part of the journey of spirituality. The miracle of the manna clearly demonstrates that God intends for his people to live one day at a time.

Living one day at a time is closely related to the necessity of traveling without a map through the uncharted territory of the wilderness of change and growth (Chapter 3). In the Exodus story, God led the Hebrews through the wilderness by assuming the form of a pillar of cloud by day and a pillar of fire by night. Thus, the Hebrews could travel by day or night as God guided them on their way to the Promised Land (Ex. 13:21). Nevertheless, the Israelites could see no further ahead on their journey than the pillar of cloud or fire that hovered before them. In other words, they could see no more than about one day's journey down the road.

Similarly, as we embark on the journey of spirituality today, we often can see no further than one day's journey ahead. Because God does not allow us to see into the future, we must live and travel one day at a time. We must journey by faith, believing that the God who sustains us today will also sustain us through the uncertainties that lie beyond the horizon.

More than Bread Alone

For the Israelites, who had wandered far into the Sinai wilderness, living one day at a time had become a matter of practical necessity. In the arid desert where food and water were scarce, they depended totally on God for survival. The raining of the manna from heaven one day at a time, both literally and metaphorically, dramatized an essential part of the journey of spirituality: it showed that God intended for his people to look to him to supply their daily needs.

God made it inescapably clear to the Hebrews that he was their provider and sustainer. He took them into the sparse, arid Sinai Peninsula so they could learn they needed more than food: they needed God. The lingering illusion of self-sufficiency (the innate desire to "run my own show" or "do it my way") quickly evaporated in the transforming heat of the wilderness. As Moses wrote years later:

> [God] humbled you, causing you to hunger and then feeding you with manna, which neither you nor your fathers had known, to teach you that man does not live on bread alone but on every

word that comes from the mouth of the LORD. Your clothes did not wear out and your feet did not swell during these forty years. Know then in your heart that as a man disciplines his son, so the LORD your God disciplines you.

(Deut. 8:3–5)

In the New Testament, in that famous discourse known as "The Sermon on the Mount," Jesus echoed the same lesson that was taught the Hebrews in the wilderness: we must depend on God to supply our needs. Jesus' magnificent words, ones that through the ages have strengthened those who travel the arduous journey of faith, merit our careful reflection. He said:

Therefore I tell you, do not worry about your life, what you will eat or drink; or about your body, what you will wear. Is not life more important than food, and the body more important than clothes? Look at the birds of the air; they do not sow or reap or store away in barns, and yet your heavenly Father feeds them. Are you not much more valuable than they? Who of you by worrying can add a single hour to his life?

And why do you worry about clothes? See how the lilies of the field grow. They do not labor or spin. Yet I tell you that not even Solomon in all his splendor was dressed like one of these. If that is how God clothes the grass of the field, which is here today and tomorrow is thrown into the fire, will he not much more clothe you, O you of little faith? So do not worry, saying, "What shall we eat?" or "What shall we drink?" or "What shall we wear?" For the pagans run after all these things, and your heavenly Father knows that you need them. But seek first his kingdom and his righteousness, and all these things will be given to you as well. Therefore do not worry about tomorrow, for tomorrow will worry about itself. Each day has enough trouble of its own.

(Matt. 6:25–34)

In this passage, Jesus talks about the basic necessities of life: food to eat, something to drink, and clothes to wear. In those days, as well as throughout all biblical times, these necessities could never be taken for granted. The water supply depended on the amount of snow in the mountains in a given year, and inadequate rainfall was common. A shortage of water affected the growth of crops (i.e., the food supply), and a shortage of crops damaged the whole economy, a fact that meant even clothes were harder to obtain.[2] Nevertheless, to people living in those precarious circumstances, to those for whom the necessities of life were never certain, Jesus said do not worry about what you will eat, what you will drink, or what you will wear.

Jesus' words are not those of a carefree hedonist who lives only to indulge in the pleasures of the present day; they are the words of one who lived only to do the will of his Father in heaven (Jn. 6:38). Both Jesus' teaching and the miracle of the manna from heaven show that living one day at a time is neither a frivolous, hedonistic manner of living, nor one wherein we stick our heads in the sand and hope that our problems go away. To the contrary, living one day at a time is a matter of trusting God to provide for us.

WORRY: BORROWING TOMORROW'S TROUBLES TODAY

Our failure to live one day at a time is no more evident than in the common tendency to worry. Worry is the bane of all those who would live one day at a time. The word *worry* comes from an old German word that means *to strangle* or *to choke*.[3] To choke means, among other things, *to check the growth or development of.* Worry, then, is a kind of mental and emotional strangulation.[4] Just as weeds choke the growing petunias in a summer garden, so worry chokes our psychological, emotional, and spiritual growth.

More than any other factor, worry chokes out the peace, serenity, and joy that might otherwise enrich our lives.

Consider, for example, Madeline, a thirty-six-year-old interior designer who came to me for counseling. Though she had had several casual relationships in the two years since her divorce, Madeline came to her fourth session excited but worried because a man in her singles Bible study group had recently invited her to dinner and a movie. The man had an excellent reputation and was considered a person of integrity by everyone in the singles group. Moreover, Madeline had long admired him from a distance because his insightful contributions to the group's discussions had convinced her that he was a sincere and dedicated Christian. When he actually asked her out, however, she was worried and fearful, and she brought her concerns to counseling. "I'm afraid that he won't like me once he gets to know me," she said. "He probably won't like any of the things I like, and he'll think I'm a complete boor. Besides," she continued, "what will he think when he finds out I'm divorced. I'll bet he won't have anything to do with me then." Later, she said that she was afraid she would say something stupid at dinner, and he would think she was an idiot. Finally, she completely convinced herself that she had no chance of a relationship with the man she so clearly admired. Madeline had become tangled in the web woven by worry. Though she had not yet had the first date with her admired friend, she was already certain that a relationship with him was impossible. Rather than live one day at a time, she had grabbed hold of the elusive future in a determined effort to wrest her worst fears from it. Clearly, worry had choked the joy out of her new relationship even before it had started.

Tom is another example of one whose worry about tomorrow brought misery into his life today. It was readily apparent that he had ceased to live one day at a time because Tom came to his counseling session obsessively worried that he was about to lose his job. Because the international communications firm that had employed him for many years had been plagued by disastrous financial losses in recent months, many long-time employees had been fired. Tom was terrified that he would be next. Even as he voiced his fears in counseling, he began to worry frantically about how he would support his wife and four children if he lost his job. Then his anxious thoughts turned to the house they lived in. The entire family loved their home, but the house had a large mortgage payment that he could not pay if unemployed even for a short time. Next, Tom began to worry about how he would pay the college tuition for his oldest son, then a senior in high school. As if all that weren't enough, Tom began to worry about what would happen if he and his family lost the medical coverage that was part of his compensation: "What if one of the boys gets seriously ill and has to go to the hospital?" he asked. Even though Tom had not lost his job, he was already suffering emotionally as though he had just joined the ranks of the unemployed. He had grabbed hold of the worst-case scenario and was obsessing over it. His anxious worry continued through the coming weeks to the point that he had to seek medical attention for what had been a dormant ulcer. To be sure, worry had sapped all the joy from Tom's life.

In addition to his useless worry, Tom's mistake was that he was not doing what he could to plan for a layoff; for example, he had not looked into the possibility of employment with another communications firm. He had merely planned for the worst and had begun to live as though it had already come true. Instead of living one day at a time, that is, doing what he could that day to plan for a layoff, he had transformed his worst fears into nightmarish dragons that he fought for his very life.

Fortunately, Tom eventually learned that he would not be laid off. Nevertheless, though his worry proved needless, it had robbed him of many nights of sleep and many days of peace. Perhaps the rest of us can learn from Tom's experience that "the future of reality is seldom as bad as the future of our fears."[5]

Worry and the Illusion of Control

Worry derives from the need for control that marks the lives of many in our insecure society. Though worry may seem to indicate that we have lost control of some aspect of our lives, paradoxically, worry is actually an attempt to gain control over something that concerns us, whether a person, event, or thing. We believe that if we fret hard enough, pace far enough, and worry long enough, we can discover some means to control people, events, and things.

When we worry about tomorrow, we try to grab hold of the future in order to bend it to our wills. In other words, worry is a way to grapple with the unforeseen events that threaten us. Thus, it allows us to feel actively involved in our lives. Nevertheless, because it allows us to feel like something more than helpless victims tossed about by the rough seas of life, worry is a sure sign that we fail to accept our finitude and human limitation. Worry, then, fosters an illusion of control over various aspects of our environments. Though Jesus taught to the contrary, many seem to believe that by worrying we can actually add a foot to our stature and an hour to our lives.

Worry is the offspring of the dragon of fear. In other words, fear breeds worry. We worry because we are afraid of what tomorrow will bring, not only to ourselves, but to our loved ones as well. For many, tomorrow seems dark and threatening, a strange and elusive phantom that remains just beyond our grasp, always evading our best efforts to manage it. To try to control tomorrow today is like wrestling a ghost: reach out to grab hold of it, and it disappears into thin air.

George MacDonald, the nineteenth-century Scottish preacher, poet, and novelist that C.S. Lewis called master, understood the futility of worrying about tomorrow today. He wrote:

> The next hour, the next moment, is as much beyond our grasp and as much in God's care, as that a hundred years away. Care

for the next minute is just as foolish as care for the morrow, or for a day in the next thousand years—in neither can we do anything, in both God is doing everything.[6]

TRUST: THE ANTIDOTE TO WORRY

According to theologian William Barclay, "Worry is essentially distrust of God."[7] Though many are reluctant to admit it, our fear-induced worries arise because we do not trust God to journey with us into the unknown territory that is tomorrow.

The lives of many in our anxiety-ridden society are characterized by a basic distrust of God. Those who grew up in dysfunctional families tend to view God as they did their parents: if their mothers and fathers or other care givers were abusive, distrustful, and uncaring, they will view God in much the same manner. Many envision God as a harsh taskmaster who impatiently seeks every opportunity to make their lives miserable. Therefore, they turn from God in hopes that he will simply leave them alone to pursue their own courses. They deceive themselves by believing they can find their own way to the promised land. Surrendering to another the all-important need for control is difficult, even when that other is God.

The people of Israel, too, were reluctant to trust God. Despite the divine miracles they had witnessed, they still doubted whether God would provide for them; thus, they grumbled because they were afraid they would starve in the desert. But it is important to note that God purposely drove the people into a harsh, sparsely vegetated region so they could learn a vital lesson: that God is a trustworthy provider. As God said just before sending the manna and quail, "At twilight you will eat meat, and in the morning you will be filled with bread. Then you will know that I am the LORD your God" (Ex. 16:12). God sent down the manna from heaven to teach the hungry Israelites they could trust the divine plan unfolding in their lives. Day after day for forty years, the bread of life rained from the heavens so they could learn that God is a dependable provider.

God is the same today as thirty-five hundred years ago; the divine sustainer does not change. God desires that his people learn to depend upon him for life itself.

Yet, we cannot both trust God and wring our hands in anxious worry at the same time. Trust and worry make poor bedfellows; they cannot coexist in the human heart. One brings peace, joy, and serenity to our lives; the other stress, doubt, and unhappiness. Trust and worry are inversely related: as one increases, the other decreases. Therefore, trust is the antidote to worry and fear.

In the Psalms, David wrote, "The LORD is my shepherd, I shall not be in want. . . . Even though I walk through the valley of the shadow of death, I will fear no evil, for you are with me; your rod and your staff, they comfort me" (Ps. 23:1,4). Even beneath the looming specter of death, David was unafraid because he trusted God to be with him. Like David, we must trust God to be with us in the arduous journey of faith.

FAITH PLUS ACTION EQUALS TRUST

As we have seen, worry is the offspring of fear. On the other hand, trust is the offspring of faith. To be sure, the kind of faith that enables us to step into the sea when called to do so encompasses far more than mere intellectual assent to theological or biblical truths. In other words, faith is more than merely saying, "I believe." Faith ultimately requires action, for without action faith is dead (Jas. 2:17). When faith couples with action, however, trust is born.

In my previous book, *The Gospel and the Twelve Steps,*[8] I paraphrased a story often told by Billy Graham to illustrate the difference between simply saying "I believe" and really trusting God in faith. The story is as follows:

A brave man pushes a wheelbarrow back and forth along a tightrope suspended high above Niagara Falls. The crowd watches in astonishment as the agile acrobat continues to push the wheelbarrow back and forth over the deadly, roaring falls. Then the man places a 200-pound sack of dirt in the wheelbarrow and boldly makes his way across the falls, pushing the heavy load through the misty air. Making his way back, the tightrope walker points to a man in the crowd and asks, "Do you believe I can push a man in the wheelbarrow across the falls?" The excited onlooker says, "Yes, of course." The acrobat points directly at the man and says, "Get in!"[9]

All who travel through the wilderness of change and growth will encounter the roaring chasms of life where God asks each of us to get into the wheelbarrow. We join our faith to action by getting in and trusting God to take us across.

CHAPTER 5

Pitfalls in the Path

There are many people who have sought light and truth, but they look for it outside themselves where it is not.

—Augustine[1]

Thus far in the Exodus story we have seen how the Israelites progressed along the path from bondage and brokenness to faith and trust. God released the people from their enslavement in Egypt. Then, at the Red Sea, God delivered them from the Egyptians when the people put themselves under his care and marched forward into the sea. Soon thereafter, when they grew hungry and feared starvation in the sparse wilderness, God again provided for the people by raining down manna, the bread from heaven. Similarly, as the Israelites camped at Rephidim, a place with no water, God once again showed faithfulness and willingness to provide when life-giving water poured from the rock of Horeb after Moses struck it with his staff (Ex. 17:1–7).

An Idol of Gold

In the third month after the Israelites left Egypt, they came to Mount Sinai and set up camp at its base (Ex. 19:1–2). Then God called from the mountaintop and Moses ascended Sinai to receive the laws of God.[2]

Moses was on the mountain communing with God for many days. As thunder roared and lightning flashed from the summit of Mount Sinai, the people waiting below grew restless and uneasy because of the prolonged absence of their leader. As the days passed, the people grew increasingly anxious and impatient because they thought that Moses, the visible representative of God, had abandoned them. They began to long for something or someone to restore a sense of order and security to their existence. According to the scriptures:

> When the people saw that Moses was so long in coming down from the mountain, they gathered around Aaron and said, "Come, make us [a god] who will go before us. As for this fellow Moses who brought us up out of Egypt, we don't know what has happened to him."
>
> Aaron answered them, "Take off the gold earrings that your wives, your sons and your daughters are wearing, and bring them to me." So all the people took off their earrings and brought them to Aaron. He took what they handed him and made it into an idol cast in the shape of a calf, fashioning it with a tool. Then they said, "[This is your god], O Israel, who brought you up out of Egypt." (Ex. 32:1–4, footnoted translation)

After only a few weeks in the wilderness of change and growth, the Israelites grew dissatisfied with God. They no longer wished to worship the one who had delivered them from Egypt, who had parted the waters of the Red Sea, and who had rained manna from heaven in response to their cries of hunger. Instead, they demanded of Aaron, "Make us a god who will go before us." Because they felt abandoned and threatened, their spirituality was overcome by sensuality. They wanted something tangible to bring relief to their anxiety and distress and to instill a renewed sense of order to their lives. No longer content to worship the unseen God, they demanded a god they could see and touch, a god that would appeal more to their senses than to their souls. Therefore, they persuaded Aaron to form a golden calf from the trinkets they had taken from the Egyptians.

When Aaron had completed the golden idol, the Israelites worshiped it; they even gave it credit for their deliverance from Egypt. The mute creature made of wood overlaid with gold was an idol born of their desire for a tangible solution to the anxieties and stresses they experienced in the wilderness of the Sinai. The people willingly and eagerly worshiped the object of their desire and invested into it their psychological, emotional, and spiritual energy. They offered sacrifices to the golden calf and celebrated the birth of their new god with indulgent revelry (Ex. 32:5–6). The ancient Israelites succumbed to the pervasive human proclivity to pervert reverence for the divine by their attempt to reduce the Creator of heaven and earth to a tangible god of more manageable proportions.

MODERN IDOLATRY

Deep within the heart of every person is a longing for God. By nature we desire to know the transcendent. We wish to commune with our Creator and enjoy his companionship, just as Adam and Eve walked closely with the Creator in the Garden of Eden (Gen. 3). The innate desire for God is expressed throughout the psalms of the Old Testament. In one particularly beautiful passage, the psalmist writes: "As the deer pants for streams of water, so my soul pants for you, O God. My soul thirsts for God, for the living God. When can I go and meet with God?" (Ps. 42:1–2).

Nevertheless, like the Israelites with their golden calf, many today no longer seek communion with the divine source of our beings. Instead, we invest our psychological, emotional, and spiritual energies into the objects of the material world. The apostle Paul clearly described this perverse tendency to worship gods of our own making rather than the Creator God of heaven. He wrote:

> For although they knew God, they neither glorified him as God nor gave thanks to him, but their thinking became futile and their foolish hearts were darkened. Although they claimed to be wise, they became fools and exchanged the glory of the immortal God for images made to look like mortal man and birds and animals and reptiles. . . . They exchanged the truth of God for a lie, and worshiped and served created things rather than the Creator—who is forever praised. Amen.
>
> (Rom. 1:21–25)

Many today look with disapproval upon the primitive practices of the Israelites or other groups who fashion idols of wood, stone, or even gold. Nevertheless, though we consider ourselves much too sophisticated for such psychologically immature practices, we, too, are idol worshipers. Our idols, however, are more cleverly disguised than primitive idols encrusted with gold and silver or bedecked with gawking eyes of emeralds or rubies. Yet though more subtle, our modern idolatry is little different from the animistic practices of many pagan peoples.

THE DRAGON OF DESIRE

Like the Israelites, whose desire for a god they could see and touch drove them into idolatry, we have sacrificed our spirituality on the altar of sensuality. Moreover, our modern idolatry is an outgrowth of our insatiable, innumerable desires.

According to the ancient philosopher Aristotle, "It is the nature of desire not to be satisfied, and most human beings live only for the gratification of it."[3] The pervasive idols of our culture are manifestations of the many-faced creature who is the second guardian of the winding path to the Temple of Life in the middle of the garden: the ravenous dragon named Desire, the seductive creature on whose every scale are emblazoned the words, "I want."[4] As surely as the path to the promised land is fiercely guarded by the awful dragon of fear, so, too, the way is guarded by the appealing dragon of desire. For many, the alluring second dragon is even more difficult to circumvent than the first.

FILLING IN THE BLANK

Like the golden calf fashioned by Aaron for the Israelites, all manifestations of the dragon of desire easily become idols—that is, objects or aspects of the created world into which we invest our psychological, emotional, and spiritual energy. These idols are pitfalls in the path of spirituality. Consequently, they block our way to the promised land of freedom and wholeness.

In the Sermon on the Mount, Jesus taught very clearly that we cannot serve both God and money (Matt. 6:24). Yet his words apply not only to money, but also to the entire arena of modern idols to which we have pledged our allegiance. Perhaps we can gain insight into our own hearts by examining his teaching in a slightly different manner. Jesus said:

> No one can serve two masters. Either he will hate the one and love the other, or he will be devoted to the one and despise the other. You cannot serve both God and _____.
> (Author's variation on Matthew 6:24)

Stop for a moment and determine how you would fill in the blank. What or whom have you elevated to a god-like position in your life and, therefore, prevents you from serving God with your whole heart? Is it alcohol, drugs, sex, gambling, food, money, a person, a relationship, power, a job or career, a position, a sport, a hobby, a material object? Whatever or whoever is inserted into the blank is an idol; regardless of what or whom that idol is, you cannot serve both it and God. As Jesus plainly said, you will love one and hate the other. Thus, you must make a conscious choice regarding what or whom your master will be.

Let us, therefore, examine several of the modern idols that compete for our allegiance and threaten to draw us from the true path of spirituality, thereby causing us to lose our way to the promised land.

MONEY: A RIVAL GOD

The famous sixteenth-century reformer Martin Luther observed that we need three kinds of conversions: "the conversion of the heart, mind, and the purse."[5] For many, the conversion of the purse or wallet is the most difficult.

"'In God We Trust' may be inscribed on American money, but the money itself usually feels more trustworthy," wrote Gerald May.[6] As a younger man, I trusted in money. I viewed money as a magic wand that could make all my troubles disappear. I believed that, with enough cash, I could solve any problem. When the events of my life did not unfold as I wanted, I used money to alter the environment (whether physical or social) more to my liking. For me, money was a powerful tool that could be used to shape my environment in accordance with the dictates of my desires. Because it provided me the illusion of control and security, money became the god I trusted.

Others use the power of money to compensate for the emptiness they feel inside. Ebenezer Scrooge, the protagonist in

Charles Dickens' *A Christmas Carol*, was obsessed by money; he was enamored of it and enslaved by his desire for it. In his youth, Scrooge forfeited the chance of a lifetime of love when his fiancée left him because he loved money more than her. As the result of his misplaced affections, he became an embittered, lonely old miser. According to psychotherapist Eugene Pascal, Scrooge used the power of money to compensate for his overwhelming feelings of worthlessness and powerlessness; that is, he used something outside himself (money) to compensate symbolically for the qualities he lacked within.[7]

Jesus understood the tremendous power that money holds. According to author Richard Foster, Jesus spoke of money more than any other subject except the kingdom of God. For Jesus, money was not morally and ethically neutral; it was not mere paper or coin to be used for good or evil purposes according to the wishes of the spender. Rather, Jesus understood money to be a powerful, rival god that competed for the allegiance of human beings.[8] Thus he said, "You cannot serve both God and Money" (Matt. 6:24c). Therefore, money is a false idol whose worship we must reject in order to worship the true God with our whole hearts.

THE TYRANNY OF THINGS

Like money, material things compete for our allegiance to God and threaten to draw us onto a false path that leads away from the promised land. Perhaps in no other aspect of human behavior is our unassuageable desire so apparent as in the realm of material goods.

Because many Americans believe that having something outside ourselves will compensate for the emptiness and insecurity we feel inside, we are dominated by the desire to possess more and more tangible things. In exchange for the illusion of increased security through money and material gain, many today sacrifice more and more personal freedom on the altar of materialism.

In the years following the Second World War, Americans looked forward to shorter and shorter workweeks, and we believed that by the 60s and 70s, we would all enjoy ample leisure time because of our twenty-hour-per-week jobs. Yet today we find the opposite has occurred: Americans are not working less; we are working more. Sixty- and seventy-hour workweeks are common. Moreover, many professionals in large Fortune 500 companies work 100-hour weeks. To be sure, many work more today simply to make ends meet; yet, many others sacrifice more and more personal freedom for purely materialistic reasons: a bigger house, a nicer car, a larger boat, a bigger television, and a diamond ring with more carats than the neighbor's. But when we work longer hours simply to earn more money to purchase even more material goods we do not need in the first place, then these things become devouring gods whose only propitiation is our freedom. Consequently, we are a nation of indentured servants who have sold ourselves to the false deity of possessions in exchange for the elusive feelings of security, self-satisfaction, and well-being.

Our obsession with things is encouraged by the advertising media, an industry that, at least in its present form, could only exist in a culture obsessed with materialism. An endless parade of radio and television commercials assures us that happiness is only a toll-free call and a credit card number away. Magazine and billboard advertisements indoctrinate us into the materialistic dogma that the good life comes from possessions: a new car, a new house, a new dress, or a bottle of single-malt Scotch. Each time we log on to the Internet, a barrage of pulsing, gyrating pop-up ads assaults us with the assurance that customer satisfaction is only a mouse-click away.

Furthermore, the advertising and marketing media seek to perpetuate a feeling of dissatisfaction by fanning the flames of discontent that rage in our hearts, until all that remains is a poisonous residue of envy. Like children with their noses pressed to the candy store window, we are invited to drool before our televisions at the lifestyles of the rich and famous with their solid gold bathtub fixtures, Rolls-Royces, and villas overlooking the sea. We are led to believe that their lives are characterized by the unending excitement of chic cocktail parties, hot romances, and thrilling adventures. What is not seen behind the cameras, however, is the unparalleled number of divorces and suicides among the rich and famous; the pervasive enslavement to cocaine, Valium, and designer drugs; and the apathy, incredible boredom, and general malaise that plague the so-called beautiful people of the world.

The desire for something new and different produces dissatisfaction with what we already have. We are like children on Christmas morning who excitedly open their boxes with new fire trucks and dolls inside, but by New Year's Day are tired of them and want other toys.

To make matters worse, the desire for more things leads us right back to fear: when we do get what we want, we are afraid of losing it; or, at least, we are afraid it will get scratched, chipped, or tarnished. As we become increasingly fearful of loss or damage to our treasured things, we guard them and cling more tightly to them. We build glass cases to protect them, or we buy policies to insure them. Eventually we become bound to the objects of our desire, possessed by our own possessions.

Our craving for things leaves us in an unhealthy condition of spiritual atrophy. Possessions produce "a cotton candy experience":[9] a few seconds of intense sweetness followed by emptiness and a craving for more. Those who worship possessions are hollow men and women, aimlessly wandering a spiritual wasteland.

The Rich Young Man

A New Testament story clearly demonstrates the power wielded by both money and possessions. The story also exposes the hidden, deleterious effects of selfish desire and how it prevented someone from embarking on the journey of spirituality.

In the book of Matthew, we read of the encounter between Jesus and a rich young man who came to him and posed an important question: "Teacher, what good thing must I do to get eternal life?" (Matt. 19:16ff).

Jesus replied, "If you want to enter life, obey the commandments."

Not certain what Jesus meant, the young man asked, "Which ones?"

Jesus said, "Do not murder, do not commit adultery, do not steal, do not give false testimony, honor your father and your mother." Jesus also admonished the young man to love his neighbor as himself. Notice that Jesus listed the last part of the Ten Commandments (recorded in Exodus 20). These are the commandments that bear directly on our relationship to our fellow human beings.

No doubt with a touch of righteous indignation, the young man replied, "All these I have kept. What do I still lack?"

Apparently this young man was very good at obeying rules. His adherence to the external requirements of the law must have been genuine because Jesus did not challenge him when he said that he had kept "all these" commandments. Yet the young man was also perceptive and, perhaps, had insight into the depths of his own corrupt heart. He knew that, even though he had met the external requirements of the law, he lacked something.

Jesus said to him, "If you want to be perfect, go, sell your possessions and give to the poor, and you will have treasure in heaven. Then come, follow me."

When the young man heard Jesus' reply, he turned his back and walked away in sadness. Why? Because he had great wealth (Matt. 19:22).

Jesus demonstrated clear insight into the nature of the rich young man's character by shrewdly structuring the conversation to show exactly where the man's heart was. Notice that when Jesus cited certain of the Ten Commandments, he left out the first four commandments, those that bear specifically on our relationship to God (You shall have no other gods before me, Ex. 20:3ff). Jesus knew intuitively that, even though the young man had the outward appearance of goodness and righteousness, inwardly the man was corrupt, for his heart was in his wallet. He was held captive by his money and possessions. While he outwardly adhered to the rules, inwardly the young man was guilty of idolatry. Like the Hebrews who fashioned a golden calf, he, too, worshiped gold, for he put his wealth before God. He was ultimately unwilling to sell all his possessions and follow Jesus because he knew in his heart that he loved gold more than God. Thus he walked away in sadness.

We must understand that the young man was not spiritually impoverished because he was rich; he was spiritually impoverished because he was an idolater. He put his wealth ahead of God; he loved cash more than Christ. He was so blinded by desire that he could not see the eternal treasure standing in front of him. He proved the words of the apostle Paul to his young friend Timothy: "For the love of money is a root of all kinds of evil" (1 Tim. 6:10a).

Jesus clearly understood the human proclivity to attach desire to wealth and possessions rather than to God. In the Sermon on the Mount, he said:

> Do not store up for yourselves treasures on earth, where moth and rust destroy, and where thieves break in and steal. But store up for yourselves treasures in heaven, where moth and

rust do not destroy, and where thieves do not break in and steal. For where your treasure is, there your heart will be also.
(Matt. 6:19–21)

In this passage, writes theologian Alister McGrath, Jesus clearly contrasts two modes of living: "the inauthentic mode of existence, based upon this world, which is transitory and temporary [i.e., storing up treasures on earth]; and the authentic mode of existence based on God himself, which involves rejection of any basis of trust in this world in order to place trust in God himself [i.e., storing up treasures in heaven]."[10] The rich young man clearly lived an inauthentic existence. Rather than trust the unseen God, he trusted his money and possessions. Like a storehouse filled with treasure riddled by rust and consumed by moths, his heart was so corrupted by selfish desire that he refused to surrender his wealth and follow Jesus even at the cost of his soul. No wonder he walked away in sadness. According to George MacDonald:

> What is with the treasure must fare as the treasure. . . . The heart which haunts the treasure house where the moth and rust corrupt, will be exposed to the same ravages as the treasure. . . . Many a man, many a woman, fair and flourishing to see, is going about with a rusty moth-eaten heart within that form of strength or beauty.[11]

Like the rich young man, many in our society, including many Christians, are going about clothed in the appearance of righteousness and goodness. As MacDonald suggests, they are "fair and flourishing to see." Nevertheless, they are idolaters because they have surrendered their hearts to the religion of materialism that dominates American culture.

To rid ourselves of our culturally sanctioned attachment to possessions may require radical behavior. To illustrate, Jesus said: "The kingdom of heaven is like treasure hidden in a field.

When a man found it, he hid it again, and then in his joy went and sold all he had and bought that field" (Matt. 13:44). There is a radical difference between the attitude of the man who sold all he had to buy the field and that of the rich young man who walked sadly away from Jesus because he had great wealth. One man would allow nothing to stand between him and the kingdom of heaven; the other man valued the things of this world to the exclusion of the kingdom of heaven. One man experienced great joy over the heavenly treasure he found; the other man walked away in sadness under the heavy burden of his earthly treasures.

The story of the rich young man is a sad tale of attachment. Psychologically, emotionally, and especially spiritually, he was nailed to his possessions by his insatiable desire. He could not free himself from his attachments, not even at the direct invitation of Jesus himself. He was consumed by his desire for the possessions and material comforts that accompanied his great wealth.

For these reasons, Jesus uttered the enigmatic statement, "[I]t is easier for a camel to go through the eye of a needle than for a rich man to enter the kingdom of God" (Matt. 19:24). There are various interpretations of these puzzling words from our Lord. One highly instructive explanation is that Jesus was referring to a gate known as "the eye of the needle," a particularly narrow entrance to the city through the wall that surrounded Jerusalem. In order for traders from faraway lands to get their camels through that small gate, the beasts had to be unloaded because the large burdens they carried made them too wide to pass through. Those of us who are weighted down by worldly goods are in much the same predicament as those camels: we cannot enter the kingdom of God (symbolized by the city of Jerusalem) until we are rid of our burdensome attachments to our possessions.

RELATIONSHIPS: MISPLACED LONGING

Money and possessions are by no means the only obstacles in our path to the promised land. Other common pitfalls in the journey of change and growth are relationships. On numerous occasions in my work as a therapist, I have seen clients drawn from their paths by poorly timed relationships. Too often, a client who is making long, rapid strides through the wilderness of change and growth stumbles by becoming entangled in a new relationship with a member of the opposite sex. Because of her new involvement, she turns her attention outside herself; hence, she is no longer able to do the important inner work that is essential to the journey of change and growth. It is noteworthy that persons who enter self-help groups based on the Twelve Steps are routinely cautioned to avoid serious relationships for at least one year. Those with experience in such programs know that poorly timed relationships can quickly bring the journey of spirituality to a grinding halt.

Relationships and Desire

As stated above, many of us search outside ourselves for a solution to the emptiness we may feel inside. Often, we look to others to provide fulfillment and bring a sense of meaning to our lives. Many in our society commonly seek both happiness and security through someone else—whether spouses, friends, or lovers.

Generally, the desire to find happiness and security in relationships is expressed in two overarching ways: 1) I want you to make me happy, and 2) I want you to take care of me. Because we seek happiness and security in them, relationships are frequently characterized by getting rather than giving. The struggle to satisfy competing wants and demands produces the conflict that commonly characterizes relationships, especially our marriages. Moreover, conflict and frustration arise because our spouses or significant others cannot give us what we desire in the innermost parts of our beings. As we shall see below, what we seek in relationships simply is not there.

We can avoid most disappointments and prevent much conflict if we let go of the expectations and demands that we bring to our relationships. In other words, we must stop seeking in others solace for our existential pain, loneliness, unhappiness, and insecurity. We must surrender the expectation that relationships provide meaning, happiness, security, self-worth, and identity. Simply stated, we must forfeit the futile hope that another person can satisfy the longing of our souls.

Beyond Relationships

Human relationships are ultimately disappointing because we seek something in them that is not there, but rather lies beyond them. Theologian Alister McGrath has used an analogy from the world of classical music that may help us understand this important point: When we hear a great work like Beethoven's *Eroica* symphony, we become aware that behind the music is a person, the composer, who, through the medium of sound, reaches out to touch us and involve us in the creative endeavor that is great art. Because of the emotion engendered by the music, the listener is caught up in the passions and concerns of the composer's life. Thus, the hearer is able to connect in some way with the person beyond the music. According to McGrath:

> The music mediates the person—it points beyond itself to its ground and basis in the person of its composer. Something—such as the sense of *Sturm und Drang* [storm and stress] in a Brahms symphony, or the deep sense of melancholy in Tchaikovsky's *Pathétique*—comes *through* the music even though it is not actually *in* the music. And as

we try to capture that sense, we find that it eludes us; it lies beyond our reach—something has been evoked but cannot be grasped. This same sense of something that is so nearly captured and yet eludes us is a characteristic feature of human relationships.[12]

In human relationships something is evoked that eludes us when we try to grasp it. Our myriad attempts to control or manage the behavior of others are but futile and frustrating efforts to grab hold of something that is not in relationships, but rather lies beyond them. Those who seek happiness and security solely in relationships are like thirsty travelers who plod toward an elusive oasis in a parched, barren land. Relationships are like a mirage in the desert: they promise satisfaction and well-being, but leave us thirsty for something which lies beyond.

Relationships point beyond themselves to the ultimate source of our souls' satisfaction. At their best, human relationships are a reflection of the ultimate relationship for which we were created, and that is a relationship with God. "Thou hast made us for Thyself," said Augustine, "and the heart of man is restless until it finds its rest in Thee."[13] We make idols of human relationships when we use them as a counterfeit substitute for a relationship with our Creator.

Because human relationships may easily deter a relationship with God, the radical detachment from money and possessions advocated by Jesus applies equally to relationships. He said, "If anyone comes to me and does not hate his father and mother, his wife and children, his brothers and sisters—yes, even his own life—he cannot be my disciple" (Lk. 14:26). Of course, Jesus did not mean that we should literally hate our closest relatives, for he taught that love is the overarching principle of the entire law of God (Matt. 22:34–40). Rather, he meant that we must allow nothing, including our most intimate relationships, to stand between him and us.

POWER: THE ILLUSION OF CONTROL

Another idol commonly worshiped in our society is power. Many believe that power—like money, possessions, or relationships—holds the key to comfort and security, that it is another means to have our own ways and to satisfy the insatiable desires of our hearts.

The desire for power is closely related to the need for control that characterizes the lives of many among us. Power nurtures the illusion of control that permeates our society. We believe that with enough power, we can bend others to our wills and shape our environments in a manner that enhances our own sense of security and well-being.

In our society, power is usually viewed exclusively in relationship to others—that is, power over others. We conceive of power in the context of one-up relationships, wherein one holds ascendancy, authority, or superiority over another. Not content with mere personal power (the ability to set personal boundaries, achieve personal goals, take care of personal needs, etc.), many seek power over their families, friends, colleagues, and fellow citizens in order to shape the environment according to their wishes.

In American culture, the amount of power held over others is a measure of greatness. Donald Trump and other chief executives of large corporate conglomerates are held in esteem in our society because they wield vast power and influence over others. To many Americans, those who possess great corporate power have ascended to god-like status.

Like money, possessions, or relationships, power is seductive and alluring. In fact, according to the story in the New Testament, power was one of the means Satan used in his failed effort to tempt Jesus after the Lord fasted in the wilderness. The tempter offered Jesus the kingdoms of the world and all their splendor, if the Lord would bow down and worship him

(Matt. 4:8–10). Because power is so seductive and attractive, many who already possess millions of dollars will labor eighteen hours a day to gain control of a budding competitor's business. In fact, I once heard a wealthy banker say, "It's not more money I'm after; it's more power." Though he already exerted considerable influence in the financial world, his desire for power remained unsatisfied.

Paradoxically, many who devote their lives to the accumulation of power and control over others are motivated by an unconscious fear of their own inadequacy. Their striving for control is compensatory: in other words, they seek to offset feelings of insecurity by garnering unto themselves financial, political, or other forms of worldly power. Many who achieve great success in the corporate, professional, or political worlds are relentlessly driven by an underlying sense of inferiority, inadequacy, and low self-esteem. What others see as their success is merely a facade to cover these hidden but compelling feelings of insecurity.

The Kingdom Use of Power

As is usually the case, Jesus' ideas about power, ascendancy, and superiority were very different from the prevailing views of contemporary society. To illustrate, he said to his disciples:

> You know that the rulers of the Gentiles lord it over them, and their high officials exercise authority over them. Not so with you. Instead, whoever wants to become great among you must be your servant, and whoever wants to be first must be your slave—just as the Son of Man did not come to be served, but to serve, and to give his life as a ransom for many.
>
> (Matt. 20:25–28)

Jesus clearly recognized the human desire to lord it over others. Yet he rejected the notion of power over others as a measure of greatness. Instead, he admonished his followers to take the role of servants.

Those of us who wish to live by the rules of the kingdom of God must undergo a radical shift in our thinking, for the rules of that kingdom are diametrically opposed to those of our increasingly secular society. In the kingdom of God, to become great, we must become servants; to be first, we must be last; to find our lives, we must lose them; and to keep something, we must give it away. In keeping with the paradoxical nature of that kingdom, if we want to be truly powerful, we must accept the inherent limitations of our humanity and turn our wills and our lives over to the care of God.

Like materialistic wealth, power is a feeble deity. It cannot, for example, prevent cancer or a heart attack. To the contrary, the stressful struggle to accumulate power and wealth only increases their likelihood. Neither can power force a spouse to be faithful nor a friend to be caring. Nor can power guarantee a long and happy life. Like money, power merely fosters the illusion of control. It is an insufficient savior, another impotent idol in a false religion.

PHANTOM DEITIES

Money, possessions, relationships, and power—the predominant idols of our culture—seem to offer so much. Yet when desire compels us to grab hold of them, we discover to our disappointment that what we thought was in them actually lies beyond them.

C.S. Lewis, probably the most popular Christian author of the twentieth-century, once spoke memorable words that he applied to books and music, yet his thoughts easily apply to money, possessions, relationships, and the quest for power. He said:

[These things are] images of what we really desire; but if they are mistaken for the thing itself, they turn into dumb idols, breaking the hearts of their worshippers. For they are not the thing itself; they are only the scent of a flower we have not found, the echo of a tune we have not heard, news from a country we have never yet visited.[14]

The dumb idols of money, possessions, relationships, and power are but mere images of the thing itself, poor substitutes for that for which our souls thirst, that for which our hearts are restless. It is a hopeless quest to seek happiness, fulfillment, and meaning in money, possessions, relationships, or power. These modern gods are phantom deities, impotent idols that conjure for their worshipers the empty illusions of false hopes and unrealizable dreams. As long as we seek happiness, fulfillment, security, self-worth, and identity at the feet of these feeble deities, we search in vain, and our misplaced reverence will be rewarded with disappointment, discontent, frustration, and, finally, bitterness.

CHAPTER 6

Surrender: Letting Go and Letting God

The spiritual journey is about letting go of more and more
of what we are holding on to.

—Joseph Campbell[1]

I n the previous chapter, we left the Israelites at the foot of
Mount Sinai, engaged in indulgent revelry around the golden
calf. Recall that the people grew anxious and discontent
during Moses' absence and began to desire a god they could see
and feel. Dissatisfied with the unseen God who had brought
them from Egypt, who had led them safely through the waters
of the Red Sea, and who had sustained them in the wilderness
with manna from heaven, they cried out for a god that appealed
to their senses rather than to their souls.

WHOEVER IS FOR THE **LORD**

To continue the story: When Moses finally came down from
the mountain after weeks of communing with God, he burned
with anger when he heard the people singing and saw them
dancing around the golden calf in idolatrous revelry. He threw

the stone tablets on which the Ten Commandments were written to the ground, breaking them into pieces. Then he took the calf that Aaron had made at the people's demand and burned it in the fire. He ground the residue into powder, scattered the dust across some standing water, and made the Israelites drink it (Ex. 32:19–20).

Because the people were running wild and had become a laughing stock to their enemies (who, no doubt, were watching from the surrounding hills), Moses stood at the entrance to the camp and cried out, "Whoever is for the LORD, come to me." The Levites, a clan of the Israelites who had remained faithful to God, rallied to his side. Moses instructed them to draw their swords. Then, at his command, the Levites went among the people and killed about three thousand of their fellow Hebrews (Ex. 32:25–28). Finally, God struck the people with a plague (v. 35). Their sickness, perhaps a direct result of drinking the gold-tainted water, typifies the soul-sickness that results from all forms of idolatry.

Moses called the Levites to his side with the rallying cry, "Whoever is for the LORD, come to me." Moses offered a clear choice to the people: either serve a feeble, man-made idol, or serve the Creator God of heaven (cf. Jos. 24:15, 1 Kgs. 18:21; Matt. 6:24). God had already made the terms of service clear to Moses by inscribing them on tablets of stone. Thus, Moses called all who were willing to come to God on God's terms.

Moses' rallying cry goes out today as well. If we are to follow the example of the faithful Levites, we must come to God on God's terms. In other words, we must totally surrender to our Creator. The massive slaughter at the foot of Sinai serves as an ominous warning to those who refuse to surrender to God. The physical death of the three thousand typifies the inevitable spiritual death of all who refuse to abandon their idols and surrender to God, the true source and sustainer of our beings.

LETTING GO AND LETTING GOD

Those who have participated in self-help groups based upon the Twelve Steps of Alcoholics Anonymous are no doubt familiar with the term *surrender*. In Twelve Step circles, surrender means turning our wills and our lives over to the care of God. In other words, those who have surrendered are no longer ruled by self-will; rather, they seek God's will in all things.

Perhaps the most succinct way to understand surrender is by the oft-cited slogan, "Let go and let God." Those who let go and let God surrender self-will; they no longer insist upon having their own ways. They release their demands and expectations, both of others and of God, and they no longer seek to control people, things, and events.

No doubt, Augustine, the great Christian thinker of the fourth-century, understood surrender as letting go and letting God. Augustine said that our hands must be empty if we are to receive the things God wants to give us. In order for our hands to be empty, we must let go of what we are holding on to. Those whose hands are empty have let go of selfish demands and expectations. They have released their hold on people, things, and events and no longer attempt to control them. Furthermore, those whose hands are empty have released their grip on the idols of our culture. They have abandoned the hopeless quest to find meaning and happiness in money, possessions, relationships, power, and the many other modern idols worshiped in our society. Those with empty hands have surrendered their demand for gods that can be seen and touched and, instead, have turned to the unseen and transcendent God of heaven. In summary, those whose hands are empty have surrendered to the divine process that orders all existence. They have let go in all aspects of their lives.

RENUNCIATION

As we saw earlier, to reach the Temple of Life in the middle of the garden, we must get past the awful dragons named Fear and Desire. In the present book, we have discussed at length how these two protean beasts guard the way to the promised land. We learned that getting past the dragon of fear requires us to take up the shield of faith and march forward on the journey, trusting God to accompany us through the arduous trials and difficulties that confront us. But what is the secret to getting beyond the dragon of desire? How can we overcome and conquer that seductive guardian of the path of spirituality?

The teachers of the world's great wisdom traditions tell us that those who wish to get past the dragon of desire must practice *renunciation*, a word that does not flow smoothly from American lips. To be sure, many think of renunciation as a radical form of detachment that requires the begging bowl, rough habit, and hemp rope of Francis of Assisi. For those who would follow the spiritual path, however, renunciation does not necessarily mean literally giving up all material comforts as did the beloved Francis; rather, it implies a *willingness* to let go of all we are holding on to.

In the previous chapter, at the conclusion of the story of the rich young man, we saw that the disciples were astonished by Jesus' words about the rich (Matt. 19:25). Nevertheless, as astounding as that proclamation was, the Lord uttered an even more radical statement: "[A]ny of you who does not give up [let go of] *everything* he has cannot be my disciple" (Lk. 14:33, emphasis added). In clear contrast to the rich young man, the man who found the treasure hidden in the field was willing to give up everything for the kingdom of heaven (Matt. 13:44). The apostle Paul also was willing to give up everything in order to gain Christ. He wrote, "I consider everything a loss compared to the surpassing greatness of knowing Christ Jesus my Lord, for whose sake I have lost all things. I consider them rubbish, that I may gain Christ" (Phil. 3:8).

Perhaps we can gain greater insight into the dramatic words of both Jesus and the apostle Paul by employing an analogy from the American West. Let us imagine that we are following a day's journey behind a wagon train headed west during the days of the American frontier. At each river crossing and at the foot of each steep mountain grade, we are shocked to find the trail littered with valuable items: a piano, a heavy trunk filled with clothes, a spinning wheel, or even a few precious, irreplaceable family heirlooms. What has happened, we wonder? Soon we realize that those determined settlers who traveled ahead of us were willing to throw out anything that weighed down their wagons and hindered their horses and oxen as the animals heaved and struggled to pull their heavy loads across the difficult places on the trail. In short, those hardy pioneers who traveled west in the rugged days of the American frontier were willing to surrender, or to let go of, everything they held dear in order to reach their new homes at the far end of the Oregon trail. Those of us who make the arduous journey of spirituality through the rugged wilderness of change and growth must be willing to do the same if we hope to reach the promised land.

Renunciation and letting go are kindred concepts. They are matters of the will and heart. They imply a willingness to surrender all to God. Therefore, to let go and let God does not necessarily mean taking a vow of poverty. Neither does it mean we are no longer allowed to enjoy the innumerable delights of the created world. Nor does it mean we are to adopt a rigid asceticism and forsake all forms of creature comfort. To the contrary, renunciation, or letting go, means that we release our grip on these things. We no longer demand or require them in order for our lives to be fulfilled. As a result, we are *free* to enjoy them because we are no longer attached to them.

In summary, renunciation is a willingness to love God more than money, possessions, relationships, and power, and to let go of all these things if that is what the love of God requires in our lives. It is noteworthy that many of the Jewish leaders who believed in Jesus were afraid to acknowledge him because they loved the praises of men more than they loved God (Jn. 12:42–43). They refused to renounce their desire for praise and admiration because the accolades of their fellows were more important to them than knowing God. Likewise, only when we love money, possessions, relationships, and power more than we love God do we stand condemned as idolaters.

LETTING GO OF OUTCOMES

To release our grip on the idols of our culture requires the recognition of the impermanence of life; that is, we must accept the fact that those things to which we cling are utterly temporal and transitory. According to my fellow therapist Ken Gilburth, there are only two constants in the universe: 1) God, and 2) change. Everything that exists (except God) is in a state of flux: Our bodies change with age, our hair turns gray, our children grow up, and loved ones pass away. Marriages begin and end, friends move to other towns, presidents come and go, and executives step down to those younger. Cars rust, dishes are broken, diamond earrings are lost, and the faithful dog dies. The shirt factory goes out of business, the old church on the corner is torn down, the paint on the house begins to peel, and a storm takes the old oak in the backyard. Even our own lives are utterly temporal and transitory, "a mist that appears for a little while and then vanishes" (Jas. 4:14).

Nonetheless, many of us have great difficulty accepting the inevitable and, often, painful changes that life brings. Though we and all things around us are in a state of flux, we do not want to accept the impermanence of life. Many find change frightening and unpredictable; thus, we seek to control our environment in order to maintain a reassuring feeling of constancy. Since we fear change, we anxiously project our feelings and thoughts into the future to try to grab hold of tomorrow and bend it according to the dictates of today's desires. As is often the case, we desperately want to control tomorrow's outcomes today.

Today's Desires, Tomorrow's Outcomes

Nowhere is our tendency to grab hold of outcomes more apparent than in the realm of desire. To be sure, many waste much energy attempting to control the future in order to ensure that it pans out according to today's wants and wishes. We invest the future with present desires and frantically try to ensure that tomorrow will pay off according to today's plans.

Our prayers clearly reveal our tendency to allow outcomes to be ruled by desire. Bewitched by our incessant wanting, we cling to our plans and wishes and frantically importune God to bring them to fruition. We pray: God, please give me the new house I want. God, please get me the promotion I want. God, please get me into the graduate school I want. God, please make this relationship work out the way I want. God, please make this business venture a success. In complete denial of our human limitation, we fall prey to the belief that we know what is best for us. Deluded by an infantile sense of omniscience, we attempt to manipulate God like a genie in a bottle compelled to grant our next three wishes.

Yet, a painful by-product results from our tendency to plan tomorrow according to what we want today—at the moment desire impels us to grab hold of outcomes, fear begins to plague us. Because we are afraid we will not get what we are certain we must have, our daily existence is plagued with worry and anxiety. What will I do if I can't get a loan for the new house? What will happen if I don't get that promotion at the office? How will

I ever land a position in a prestigious firm if I don't get accepted into Harvard Law School? How will I ever be happy if she doesn't return my love? What if my business venture fails; how will I pay the bills? Because tomorrow is invested with today's demands and expectations, our lives are marked by fear, worry, and anxiety at the high cost of peace, serenity, and contentment.

The apostle Paul wrote, "Do not be anxious about anything, but in everything, by prayer and petition, with thanksgiving, present your requests to God. And the peace of God, which transcends all understanding, will guard your hearts and your minds in Christ Jesus" (Phil. 4:6–7). The peace of God which transcends all understanding comes only to those who let go of outcomes and leave the future in the capable hands of God.

As we begin to think about letting go of outcomes—and exactly how one does that—many questions may come to mind. Since we cannot control tomorrow's outcomes today, should we take no thought for the future? If we are not to worry about tomorrow, should we make no plans for the future? Since we are to live one day at a time, does that mean it is wrong to make provision for tomorrow? For example, is it wrong to save money for retirement or plan for our children's college needs? These are valid questions that concern those who wish to travel the spiritual path.

Making plans for the future is certainly not wrong. As Jesus indicated, one should estimate the cost before building a tower (Lk. 14:28). Intelligent planning requires us both to evaluate our skills and talents to see if we have the ability to carry out our plans and to tally our assets to see if we have adequate resources to bring our plans to fruition. Therefore, wisdom and prudence call for making plans and preparations for the future.

In the passage from the Sermon on the Mount quoted at length earlier in this book (Chapter 4), Jesus did not say take no thought about the future; rather, he cautioned us to take no *anxious* thought about the future (Matt. 6:34).[2] Jesus did not say, "Forget about tomorrow." He said, "Do not *worry* about tomorrow." Those who follow his teaching by letting go of outcomes and placing them into the hands of God are free of the fear and anxiety that worry about tomorrow brings.

No Concern for the Harvest

The essence of letting go of outcomes is expressed beautifully in the writings of two ancient Eastern texts. According to author Robert Doran, the *Bhagavad Gita* speaks of acting but renouncing the fruits of our actions, and the *I Ching* advises, "If one does not count on the harvest while plowing or on the ground while clearing it, it furthers one to undertake something."[3] To plow a field without counting on the harvest is the epitome of letting go of outcomes; it is the meaning of renunciation.

At a small-group discussion many years ago, I heard someone describe what I think is the best way to resolve the tension between making plans for the future and letting go of outcomes. She said, "Make plans, but don't plan the outcome." To be sure, even the farmer who plows a field with no concern for the harvest must make plans. He does not simply throw a handful of seeds on the ground and hope for the best. To the contrary, after plowing and planting, he must continue to prepare the field by using pre-emergent herbicides to reduce the growth of weeds among the crops. Then, after the young plants have broken through the surface, he must judiciously apply pesticides to protect the emerging plants from ravenous insects. In other words, the farmer uses his knowledge, expertise, and his varied equipment in a planned effort to ensure a bountiful harvest. Once he has completed his various tasks, however, the outcome of his labor is largely out of his hands. His crops depend upon proper amounts of sunshine and timely rains. Too much sunshine and not enough rain can burn up his hopes for a bountiful harvest (in times of drought, even irrigation may be impossible); too little sunshine and too much rain can foil not only his plans for the harvest, but can inundate his fields and even flood his house and the neighboring town, a misfortune shared by thousands of Midwesterners in the summer floods of recent years. Moreover, swarms of locusts or other insects may sweep down to gorge themselves on what may have been otherwise a bumper crop. Therefore, the farmer who plows with no concern for the harvest is one who uses his skills and expertise to plan for a productive outcome, but beyond that takes no anxious thought for the harvest. Worrying about the outcome of his labor will not increase the growth of a single plant in the field, nor will it ensure that the crop will come in as he hopes. The farmer's task is to plan the harvest and to work the field he is given. The outcome of his plans and efforts is in the hands of God.

Like the farmer, each of us has a part to play in the events that affect our lives. We must make prudent plans for our futures. But after we have plowed our fields of endeavor, planted the seeds, and exercised the options available to us, we must turn matters over to the care of God. The farmer does not know if the rain will come to water the seeds so they will germinate, or if an early frost will kill the crop just before the harvest. Likewise, we do not know if our important business venture will succeed, or if it will fail because of government cutbacks in our industry or a reversal in the stock market. Similarly, we do not know if the money we have diligently saved for a retirement home in the mountains will be used to build a cabin or to pay excess hospital costs because of a catastrophic illness. Moreover, we do not know if our relationships will last, if our children will grow up healthy and strong, or if all our plans will be cut short by a heart attack or a fatal car crash. These things are beyond our control.

What, then, is the secret to plowing a field without counting on the harvest? How can we act while renouncing the fruits of our actions? How do we make plans but not plan the outcome? The answer is: *We do what we can, and leave to God what we can't.* We work the field, then leave the harvest in divine hands. We surrender to God the fruits of our actions. We surrender to God our insistence upon certain outcomes. As said in Twelve Step programs, we turn our wills and our lives over to the care of God. In short, we let go and let God!

Among the persons I know who practice the manner of living described above, one who stands out in my mind is Sister Clare Van Lent. She is the director of the Dwelling Place,[4] a Franciscan prayer center in my state. Sister Clare is an inspiring example of a woman who lives by faith, not by sight.

From its beginning the Dwelling Place has had no predictable source of income for its operations. With little or no financing from institutions or foundations, the center depends largely on the income from retreatants and the gifts and offerings of those who wish to contribute to its ministry. Clare once told me that, in times past, she had devised her own plans to raise funds for her ministry of prayer and solitude. She had planned seminars and had advertised them in local newspapers to get the word out about the center. She had written grant requests to raise money to fund its operations. But in every case, her efforts had come to zero. Not once, she told me, had her efforts to expand the ministry directly resulted in an increase in either the number of retreatants at the prayer center or in the amount of contributions to it. Finally, God told her to "stand aside" (her words) and he would provide for the ministry.

Today, the center continues to grow, and additional housing is under construction. How does the ministry flower even though the efforts of Clare and other personnel seem to have few direct results? Perhaps the following incident will convey the answer to that question. A few years ago, the sisters of the Dwelling Place were in need of a thousand dollars to pay for the surveying of a new facility they wished to construct at the center. Payment for the service was due the next day, and as is typical of Catholic nuns, they had no money. That morning, Clare went to the mailbox and, probably not to her surprise, found an envelope that contained a check for one thousand dollars. The money came "out of the blue," she said, from an unlikely source. Such is but one of numerous examples of God's timely provision for the ministry of the Dwelling Place. According to Sister Clare, those who really trust God to provide do not have to plow their own fields; God will do even that. As she said, "All we may need to do is go out and stir up the dirt every now and then."

In the final analysis, the journey of spirituality is about letting go of more and more of what we are holding on to. That is the meaning of renouncing the fruits of our actions, of plowing a field with no concern for the harvest. To be sure, that has been the manner of living both taught and practiced by the staff of the Dwelling Place. It is also the manner of living that characterizes the lives of those who have surrendered to God and trust him to care and provide for them.

LETTING GO OF SELF-SUFFICIENCY

> Now listen, you who say, "Today or tomorrow we will go to this or that city, spend a year there, carry on business and make money." Why, you do not even know what will happen tomorrow. What is your life? You are a mist that appears for a little while and then vanishes. Instead, you ought to say, "If it is the Lord's will, we will live and do this or that."
> (Jas. 4:13–15)

One of the great illusions of our society, one that plagues many Americans, is the illusion of self-sufficiency. In a culture that worships the rugged individualist, we cling to the false belief that we possess all the resources necessary to bring peace, joy, and meaning to our lives. We sternly admonish each other, "Pick yourself up by the bootstraps!" "Never admit defeat!" To disavow human limitation, we delude ourselves with the uniquely American cliché, "Anything is possible if you put your mind to it." With giddy laughter and "high-fives" all around, we heroically build cardboard castles with make-believe moats to protect ourselves against the frightening forces that besiege us: anxiety, alienation, loneliness, hopelessness, and the ever-looming specter of death.

The desire to escape death and ensure our own immortality has characterized human existence since the beginning. From the time of Adam and Eve, we have been seduced into all manners of destructive behaviors by our desire to escape the confines of a temporal, transitory existence. In the story of the Fall, found in the Old Testament book of Genesis, the serpent deceived our first parents and enticed them to disobey God. The cunning serpent was well aware of the human desire to escape death, and he used it as a means of seduction. Therefore, the serpent told the first and perhaps greatest lie: "You will not surely die" (Gen. 3:4).

But as great as that lie was, the serpent did not stop there. He immediately attacked our first parents at another vulnerable side of human nature: he told them they would be like God (Gen. 3:5). Alister McGrath writes, "It is clear that a major element in the story of the Fall (Genesis 3) concerns the desire on the part of humanity to dispense with God in order to become self-sufficient."[5] Moreover, "Genesis 3 makes it clear that the fundamental sin of humanity lies in denying its creaturely status and attempting to become self-sufficient, placing itself in the place of God its creator."[6] The serpent appealed to the corrupt human desire to be self-sufficient rather than dependent on the Creator. According to McGrath, the attempt at self-sufficiency is what both the Old and New Testaments call "sin."[7]

Both the wish for self-sufficiency and the related desire to dispense with God are rooted in our infantile egocentricity and sense of omnipotence. Our natural, unregenerated predisposition is to eschew the need for God. At heart, we are like the four-year-old child who defiantly shouts to his or her parents, "Leave me alone; I can do it myself!" In our desire for independence and self-determination, we have turned away from God and have sought fulfillment in money, possessions, relationships, power, and the other modern idols of our culture.

The New Testament challenges this inauthentic mode of existence. The Scriptures admonish us to abandon all security created by ourselves and trust, instead, in the sufficiency of Jesus Christ. As Professor McGrath states:

> Instead of clinging to transitory things for security, we learn to abandon faith in this transitory world in order that we may place our trust in something eternal—God himself. . . . Instead of denying the reality of our human finitude and the inevitability of death, we recognize that these have been faced and conquered through the death and resurrection of Jesus Christ, whose victory becomes our victory through faith.[8]

The apostle Paul learned to be sufficient in Christ. No longer deceived by the illusion of self-sufficiency, Paul had abandoned faith in this transitory world. He had stopped clinging to things such as money, possessions, relationships, and power in order to ensure a measure of security in his life. To the Christians at Philippi, he wrote:

> I have learned to be content whatever the circumstances. I know what it is to be in need, and I know what it is to have plenty. I have learned the secret of being content in any and every situation, whether well fed or hungry, whether living in plenty or in want.
>
> (Phil. 4:11–12)

Paul's words are even more remarkable when we realize that he wrote them while under house arrest and physically chained to a Roman guard twenty-four hours a day.

Psychologically, emotionally, and spiritually, Paul was like a self-sustaining city that had no need of imports: he was independent of external circumstances.[9] His words are a perfect description of what the medieval Christian mystics called *indifference*: for Paul, there was no difference between riches and poverty, health or sickness, feast or famine, long life or short. He had transcended the tension of opposites that characterizes the daily lives of the rest of us, leaving us torn between circumstances as they are and circumstances as we want them to be. Paul had reached a state of psychological, emotional, and spiritual wholeness in which he could remain content no matter what the opportunities or limitations of the moment.

Moreover, his words imply that he had learned the secret of contentment through a long, arduous process of initiation.[10] The trials and tribulations he had endured in his life of service to the Lord Jesus Christ had initiated Paul into the secret of contentment in all circumstances: he had been beaten, flogged, and imprisoned; he had been shipwrecked three times and had been threatened both by bandits and his own countrymen; he had been stoned and often had gone without sleep; he had known both hunger and thirst, and had been cold and naked in his mission as the apostle to the Gentiles (2 Cor. 11:23–27). Because he had descended many times into the ashes of life, Paul had learned the limitations of his own abilities. He recognized his need for a power greater than himself to sustain him. In his letter to the church at Philippi, Paul revealed the secret to his ability to remain content in all circumstances. He wrote, "I can do everything through him [Jesus] who gives me strength" (Phil. 4:13). The secret to Paul's strength and the sustaining source of his contentment was his relationship to Jesus Christ. Paul no longer depended on external circumstances because

Christ supplied all his needs. Thus, Paul was not self-sufficient; he was sufficient in Christ.

Both painfully aware of his human limitation and bolstered by his sufficiency in Christ, Paul had let go of outcomes; he had renounced the fruits of his own actions. He wrote:

> For to me, to live is Christ and to die is gain. If I am to go on living in the body, this will mean fruitful labor for me. Yet what shall I choose? I do not know! I am torn between the two: I desire to depart and be with Christ, which is better by far; but it is more necessary for you that I remain in the body. Convinced of this, I know that I will remain, and I will continue with all of you for your progress and joy in the faith, so that through my being with you again your joy in Christ Jesus will overflow on account of me.
>
> (Phil. 1:21–26)

Paul clearly had a preference (not a demand) in regard to the outcomes that confronted him. He was ready to die at the hands of the Roman guards in order to depart and be with Christ, an outcome that he regarded as far better. But for the progress and joy of the Christians at Philippi, he knew it was better to remain alive. For Paul, either outcome was advantageous: "To live is Christ": he could continue to preach the gospel (if only to the soldiers who guarded him—Phil. 1:12–13); "to die is gain": he could then be with his beloved Lord.

According to theologian and philosopher Robert Doran, "Mystics of various traditions speak of a state of detachment from inner states and outer objects, where detachment is not unrelatedness but free, non-demanding relatedness, where one is no longer preoccupied with compulsive plans . . . because one lives from that deeper center where the soul is at one with God."[11] Certainly the apostle Paul was no longer preoccupied with compulsive plans, nor was he attached to inner states (bliss, ecstasy, spiritual highs, etc.) or outer objects (money, relationships, possessions, power). Because he had surrendered his will and his life to God, Paul was "enabled to forge his life and his work with all the energy at his disposal, and at the same time to give his life and his work over to God and to let God do with it whatever he chooses, making no demands at all."[12] Paul's state of non-demanding detachment enabled him to pursue his course as apostle to the Gentiles if that was God's will or to contentedly die and be with Christ if that was the divine plan. Paul was content with either possibility because he had turned his will and his life over to the care of God. Because he had renounced the fruits of his actions and had let go of outcomes, he was able both to involve himself fully in life—even amidst suffering—and to remain contentedly detached without anxiety, expectations, or demands.

Paul's approach to life was very different from the philosophy of our control-obsessed society. Whereas we Americans usually try to control outcomes by covering all our bases, Paul had learned that the secret to contentment lay in keeping all his bases open.

SURRENDER OF SELF

We garner further insight into Paul's secret to contentment and non-demanding detachment by examining an enigmatic statement he wrote in a letter to the church at Galatia. Paul said, "I have been crucified with Christ and I no longer live" (Gal. 2:20a). When Paul says "I" have been crucified, he refers to the death of his selfish, demanding ego.

Earlier in this book, we learned that to get past the dragon of desire, we must let go of our attachments; that is, we must rid ourselves of our incessant wanting. Simply stated, we must get rid of the "want" in "I want." Yet, to attain the serene contentment enjoyed by the apostle Paul, we must also get rid of the "I." Like Paul, we must rid ourselves of our selfish, demanding egos.

His Majesty the Baby

In our natural state, there is within each of us a sinful nature that is hostile to the divine will and in active rebellion against God (Rom. 8:5–8; Gal. 5:17). Our sinful nature may be represented as an infantile, selfish despot that tolerates no frustration, brooks no delay of gratification, and reverences no master—including God. Sigmund Freud descriptively labeled this inner highchair tyrant "his majesty the baby," the metaphorical embodiment of our innate egocentricity, grandiosity, and false sense of omnipotence. His majesty's latent cries resound within each of us as he pounds his spoon upon his highchair and screams, "I want! I want! I want!"

In his boundless egocentricity, his majesty the baby views himself as the center of a personally constructed universe. He regards himself as the principal actor in the unfolding drama of life and all others as mere extras who exist solely to support him in his starring role. He is completely narcissistic. Both selfish and unloving, his pretensions of love are highly conditional and demanding. He is forever complaining, never satisfied, and always manipulating others to get what he wants.

His majesty the baby is responsible for our obsessions with money, possessions, relationships, power, and the other idols of our culture. His desire for material goods is insatiable; his thirst for power and control is unassuageable; and his unparalleled narcissism is responsible for the selfish expectations that characterize many relationships. Everyone is plagued by this inner despot or tyrannical king, and his presence is especially evident in the need for control, inability to tolerate frustration, and narcissistic demands that characterize our attitudes and feelings.

A Change of Command

His majesty the baby tolerates no competitors for his regal throne, not even God. In fact, the fundamental and most tragic flaw of this infantile egocentricity is the pervasive human desire to be god in the place of God. We have all, at varying times, succumbed to the pervasive human desire to banish God from the throne of heaven and reign in place of the divine. Our innate desire to remain on the throne of our lives is relevant to our discussion of surrender, renunciation, and letting go of self-sufficiency. Dr. Harry Tiebout, a psychiatrist who worked with alcoholics for many years, identified two internal realities that had been changed in his patients who had surrendered in their battle against alcoholism. One was the sense of omnipotence and the other was the egocentricity that characterizes human nature.[13] He learned from observing his patients that surrender involved letting go of 1) the sense of omnipotence [I am in control!], 2) the inability to tolerate frustration [I want what I want when I want it!], and 3) the expectation of immediate satisfaction of needs and wants [I want it now!]. "Dr. Tiebout believed that what had been profoundly changed in what [one of his patients] called *surrender* was that inner sense of omnipotence, that omnipotent ego. [The patient] accepted the reality of powerlessness and human limitation . . . Her delusion of omnipotence was shattered. Its dominating strength was diminished. The omnipotent ego had been dethroned."[14]

To be sure, the omnipotent ego—what we have called "his majesty the baby"—abdicates the throne only after "a sufficient degree of pain."[15] Then a new ruler may ascend the throne in our lives. In this sense, surrender is more than letting go of what we are holding on to; surrender is a change of command. This aspect of surrender is closely related to the theological term *conversion*. "The mark of conversion in the Christian faith is the confession that 'Jesus is Lord.' That means that there is a new occupant on the throne."[16]

Death Before Life

Before Jesus may be enthroned in our lives, however, a death must occur: the old king, his majesty the baby, must die. It is a spiritual principle that death *precedes* life. We see this principle enacted in nature: a seed must be buried in the ground before new life springs from it. Therefore, as surely as winter comes before spring, the old selfish, incessantly demanding ego must die before we can walk in newness of life. Jesus said, "[W]hoever loses his life for my sake will find it" (Matt. 10:39). In terms of the Christian drama, the cross precedes the resurrection.

One of Hollywood's greatest portrayals of the universal drama of death before life was the movie *Dances with Wolves*. Near the beginning of that film, the wounded Union soldier (played by Kevin Costner) mounts a horse and gallops alone toward the enemy troops. In what appears to be a suicide attempt, Costner's character repeatedly rides the length of the enemy line, allowing the Confederate soldiers to take potshots at him. Finally, in a particularly moving slow-motion scene, the hero releases the reins of his galloping horse and extends his arms wide, apparently welcoming imminent death. Leaning back in the saddle, eyes closed, arms extended wide, he resembles a man crucified on a cross. He is not killed, however, as his troops, in response to his desperate act, rally and attack.

The soldier's deed is viewed as a heroic act by his superiors, and he is offered the post of his choosing. His daring act—the total surrender of his own life and symbolic crucifixion under fire—is the vehicle by which he finds a new life among the Plains Indians. It is also the means by which he finds himself. For the Christian, the lesson is plain: we must be willing to let go of the life we had planned in order to receive the life that God has planned for us.[17] Or, as Jesus so succinctly put it, "[W]hoever loses his life for me will find it" (Matt. 16:25).

Let us now continue Paul's enigmatic statement to the Galatians:

> I have been crucified with Christ and I no longer live, but Christ lives in me. The life I live in the body, I live by faith in the Son of God, who loved me and gave himself for me.
> (Gal. 2:20)

Paul's selfish, demanding ego had died; it had been "crucified with Christ." Then he added, "I no longer live, but Christ lives in me." We see, then, that the purpose of his renunciation of self was to allow Christ to take its place. Self had died, and the Lord Jesus now lived and ruled in Paul. The apostle was then able to participate joyfully even amidst the sorrows of life because ego was no longer his center of reference; Christ was.

A Word of Caution

Pastor John Keller reminds us that "in the conversion talked about by Jesus and in the letters of St. Paul, although there is something new, the old remains. Conversion does not result in the elimination of the omnipotent ego and egocentricity."[18] To completely surrender to God our infantile sense of egocentricity and omnipotence is a difficult task, one that will take a lifetime, or more. A common problem is that we do not always want to surrender our egocentricity and sense of omnipotence. We do not wish to abdicate the throne to anyone, including God. Rather than bury our old egocentric identities, we attempt to live two lives at once by practicing our new God-centered life while clinging unrelentingly to vestiges of our old selves. We want to follow the example of Jesus, yet run our own show at the same time. It is as though we wish to live both in the light and in the dark at once, to walk precariously with one foot on either side of a line. But the line that is drawn through our hearts at conversion is, in reality, a great chasm, the wide gulf that separates those who are God-centered from those who are self-centered. As such, it cannot be crossed back and forth with impunity. Those who have experienced spiritual rebirth—that is, who have died to self and have been born again as "new creations" in Christ (2 Cor. 5:17)—have passed from death into life. Therefore, we cannot have it both ways. We cannot walk in the light and in the dark at the same time; we cannot serve two masters. We must remain on guard and continue to watch for lingering evidence of our innate selfishness and egocentricity, for like a cat with 900 lives, his majesty the baby continues to rear his ugly head, hoping to usurp his old throne. His awakening becomes apparent when we insist on having more and more things. His presence is felt when we burden others with the responsibility to make us happy or take care of us. His cries are echoed in our demands to have our own way. His stirring is sensed in our need for the approval of our peers. He is heard pounding his spoon on the highchair when we attempt to gain power over others, or when we desire to achieve status and position among our fellow humans. And again, his presence is plainly evidenced in our posturing and desire to appear to others in ways that do not mirror our inner attitudes, feelings, and beliefs.

Therefore, his majesty the baby—the selfish, demanding ego—must be put to death *daily*. The Christian drama of crucifixion followed by resurrection to new life is an ongoing one. The ancient battle between the flesh and the spirit is fought every day, one day at a time. Thus Paul writes, "I die every day" (1 Cor. 15:31). As Pastor John Keller states, "Surrender is a process, not an event."[19]

IN SUMMARY

Surrender implies that a war has been fought and one side has capitulated. In Paul's framework, this war is the ancient battle between the flesh and the Spirit; that is, between our sinful human natures and the Spirit of God whom we receive upon our conversion to the way of Christ. This war, one that is fought daily, can also be described as a struggle between two kings: 1) his majesty the baby (the innate, selfish human nature) and 2) the Lord Jesus Christ. Jesus taught that we cannot serve two masters; thus, only one king will rule our lives. For those who are Christians, that ruler must be Jesus Christ; not the inner tyrant who pounds his spoon on the highchair and screams, "I want." Therefore, this war is an ongoing struggle for rulership, for the right to be in control of our lives. We must relinquish control to the divine will if we are to attain serenity and the peace of God that transcends all understanding. Furthermore, surrender means that we must abandon the various strategies we employ to bring a (false) sense of security and well-being to our lives:

- First, we must forsake the dominant religion of our culture: materialism. We must give up the search for safety and control through the accumulation of money and possessions. To borrow George MacDonald's words, we must "get rid of the tyranny of things."[20]

- Second, we must stop trying to control others in an effort to meet our needs and wants. We must surrender both the demands and the expectations of happiness and security that we bring to our relationships. We must seek the satisfaction of our souls' longings in that which lies beyond human relationships: God.

- Third, we must stop trying to control the future by worrying today. We must let go of outcomes by renouncing the fruits of our actions; we must plow our fields and trust the harvest to God.

- Fourth, we must surrender self-will. We must forfeit the right to be in charge of our own lives; we must surrender the very right to ourselves. As Paul said, "You are not your own; you were bought at a price" (with the blood of the Christ—1 Cor. 6:19b–20a). In terms familiar to those in Twelve Step programs, we must take Step Three: turn our wills and our lives over to God.

- Fifth, and finally, we must surrender our ever-demanding egos to God. We must allow the Lord Jesus Christ to redefine us by granting him entry at the deepest level of our beings. Rather than remain the center of reference, the ego must be subordinated to God. Sigmund Freud uttered the famous maxim, "Where id was, there ego will be." As Christians, we must go beyond Freud's prescription for health and wholeness; we must be able to say, "Where ego was, there Christ will be." The founders of Alcoholics Anonymous, who clearly understood the need to surrender to God at the deepest level, wrote: "God, I offer myself to Thee—to build with me and to do with me as Thou wilt. Relieve me of the bondage of self, that I may better do Thy will."[21]

Thus, surrender is a broad concept that encompasses all aspects of our lives. Moreover, surrender is a lifelong process, wherein we give ourselves over to God's vision for us as God molds and shapes us into vessels to be used for divine purposes. And though we cannot attain perfection in this life, we can remain content with progress as we seek the divine will for our lives and surrender to God one day at a time, trusting God to forgive us where we fail and to give us the strength we need each day to continue the journey toward healing, restoration, and wholeness.

CHAPTER 7

Living in the Wilderness

So Jacob was left alone, and a man wrestled with him till daybreak.

—The Book of Genesis

In the previous chapter, we saw that the recalcitrant Hebrews refused to surrender to God on God's terms; instead, they chose to worship the golden calf, an idol of their own making. Then, when Moses returned from the summit of Sinai and saw the people singing and dancing around their newly created god, he burned with anger and called out to all those who were for the Lord. The faithful Levites rallied to him, and at Moses' command, drew their swords and slew three thousand of their fellow Hebrews.

A FAMILIAR REFRAIN

After that terrible incident, the Israelites remained at Mount Sinai for about one year. During that time they constructed the tabernacle, a portable temple that represented the house of God and could be transported as they traveled (Ex. 35:4–40:38).

Finally, God commanded the people to leave Mount Sinai and continue their journey toward Canaan, the land flowing with milk and honey.

After only a few days on their renewed journey, a familiar refrain arose: they began to complain about the manna from heaven, the food God had provided each day since they grew hungry soon after entering the wilderness. According to the Scriptures:

> The rabble [foreigners and slaves] with them began to crave other food, and again the Israelites started wailing and said, "If only we had meat to eat! We remember the fish we ate in Egypt at no cost—also the cucumbers, melons, leeks, onions, and garlic. But now we have lost our appetite; we never see anything but this manna!"
>
> (Num. 11:4–6)

Once again the dragon of desire hindered their journey to the Promised Land. Because they had grown tired of the manna, the Israelites wailed for the limited, modest diet of their days in bondage. Once again, their selective memories transformed their recollections of Egypt; thus, they began to long for the past. The hardships of the journey through the wilderness of change and growth caused them to forget the misery of slavery. Because of their difficulties, the Israelites threatened to abandon their journey to the land of milk and honey.

We must remember that the Exodus story is also our story. Like the Israelites, when the going gets rough in the wilderness of change and growth, we begin to think of returning to bondage. Whether we struggle to stay free of a dysfunctional relationship, enslavement to drugs or alcohol, or a job we hate, there comes a time when the familiar misery of the past seems preferable to the present hardships of the journey of change and growth.

To continue the story, God heard the complaining and wailing of the Israelites and said to Moses:

Tell the people: "Consecrate yourselves in preparation for tomorrow, when you will eat meat. The LORD heard you when you wailed, 'If only we had meat to eat! We were better off in Egypt!' Now the LORD will give you meat, and you will eat it. You will not eat it for just one day, or two days, or five, ten or twenty days, but for a whole month—until it comes out of your nostrils and you loathe it—because you have rejected the LORD, who is among you, and have wailed before him, saying, 'Why did we ever leave Egypt?'"

(Num. 11:18–20)

Because they were dissatisfied with what God had provided them, the Israelites succumbed to the "if only's": "If only we had meat to eat." They said, "We were better off in Egypt." As is often the case, the creature thinks it knows better than the Creator.

Like the Hebrews, all who journey through the wilderness of change and growth sometimes become dissatisfied with the way God manages our affairs. Sometimes, we think we know better than God what we need. Yet, like the Israelites who found themselves standing in quail up to their elbows (Num. 11:31), we may learn to loathe the very things we were so insistent upon having. As they say in many self-help groups, "Be careful what you ask for: you might get it!"

STILL SPIRITUAL CHILDREN

About two years after leaving Egypt, the Israelites camped at a place called Kadesh in the Desert of Paran, near the border of Canaan, the land flowing with milk and honey. Moses selected twelve men for a reconnaissance mission and ordered them to investigate the land of Canaan, its inhabitants, and their fortifications. After more than a month, the spies returned with a gloomy report for their fellow Hebrews. They claimed that the inhabitants of the land were of great size; they said the Israelites were like grasshoppers in comparison to the giants of Canaan (Num. 13). When the people heard this frightening report, they raised a refrain that had become all too familiar to Moses:

> That night all the people of the community raised their voices and wept aloud. All the Israelites grumbled against Moses and Aaron, and the whole assembly said to them, "If only we had died in Egypt! Or in this desert! Why is the LORD bringing us to this land only to let us fall by the sword? Our wives and children will be taken as plunder. Wouldn't it be better for us to go back to Egypt?" And they said to each other, "We should choose a leader and go back to Egypt."
> (Num. 14:1–4)

"Wouldn't it be better for us to go back to Egypt?" they said. Once again, when confronted by the dragon of fear, they wanted to turn back. In spite of all the miracles and divine interventions they had witnessed, the people trembled with fright at the report of the giants in Canaan. As they had at the shore of the Red Sea, the people feared they were about to perish at the hands of a powerful foe.

Those of us who read about the doubting Israelites may gawk in astonishment at their lack of faith. We think that had we witnessed the miracles and divine interventions they had seen, we would never doubt God, but, rather, would remain bulwarks of faith in the face of any foe. Let us not fool ourselves, however; their story is our story. Because the journey is difficult, painful, and frightening, many of us today who travel through the wilderness of change and growth will think of giving up and returning to the familiar misery of bondage; the days of our doubting will number many more than we will care to remember at the far end of the journey.

When the Israelites threatened to rebel because of their fear of the Canaanites, God said to Moses, "How long will these people treat me with contempt? How long will they refuse to believe in me, in spite of all the miraculous signs I have performed among them?" (Num. 14:11). In spite of all the miracles God had performed on their behalf, the people of Israel still lacked the mature faith and trust that would have enabled them to enter the land of Canaan and conquer all that opposed them. The Canaanites seemed like unconquerable giants because the Israelites were still spiritual children.

Because of their spiritual immaturity, evidenced by their lack of faith and unwillingness to surrender to the divine plan for their lives, God turned the Israelites away from the land of milk and honey. He commanded Moses to lead them back into the wilderness, where they would remain wandering pilgrims until all adult members of that unfaithful generation perished (Num. 14:26–35). Thus, for forty years after leaving Egypt, the nation of Israel underwent a time of trial and transformation in the area known today as the Sinai Peninsula.

WRESTLING WITH GOD

So Jacob was left alone, and a man wrestled with him till daybreak. When the man saw that he could not overpower him, he touched the socket of Jacob's hip so that his hip was wrenched as he wrestled with the man. . . . Then the man said, "Your name will no longer be Jacob, but Israel, because you have struggled with God and with men and have overcome."

(Gen. 32:24–25, 28)

The outward transformation of the Israelites in their long tenure in the wilderness of the Sinai mirrors the inner transformation we must undergo in the wilderness of change and growth, a transformation of the heart that results from an intimate and, often, difficult encounter with God. The wilderness of change and growth provides the context wherein an encounter with the divine is possible.

To encounter the living God is to confront the divine will at every bend in our spiritual journeys. Those who encounter God in the wilderness of change and growth find him waiting patiently at every place of decision in our daily lives, sleeves rolled up, inviting us to wrestle over the moral, ethical, and spiritual dilemmas that constantly challenge us.

Moreover, even as we climb higher toward spiritual maturity, God never leaves us resting for long at each new spiritual plateau. We barely catch our breath before God goads us onward once again toward greater spirituality. Like a seasoned mountain guide, God waits a little farther up the slope, waving his arm for us to climb toward him. But although the resting places on the ascent toward wholeness are few and far between, the attainment of ever-greater spiritual heights affords us a more encompassing view, one that opens life to us as we gain a clearer perspective on the divine will for our lives. Thus, God stretches the limits of our shortsighted faith and challenges us to an ever-increasing spiritual vision.

As we contend with God over the issues that confront us, we experience psychological, emotional, and spiritual distress, for those who wrestle with God must confront issues whose resolutions are often difficult, painful, and costly. The corporate executive who seeks the will of the divine will wrestle with God when called to give up his six-figured salary as CEO of a large tobacco company. The senior vice-president of the international savings and loan company will contend with God when her board of directors authorizes loans to murderous African dictators. The young health care worker in the ghetto clinic will wrestle with God when her supervisor orders her to assist with a third-trimester abortion. The school teacher will struggle with God when he is ordered to remove his Bible from the classroom. The unmarried president of the Christian student union will wrestle long and hard with God when she learns she is pregnant. The middle-aged woman whose husband suddenly leaves her for someone younger will wrestle with God as she cries "Why?" in the middle of a tear-filled night. The young wife and mother who learns her husband has cancer will contend mightily with God, and the parents who bury their child will cry out to God in heart-wrenching bewilderment.

Those who have contended with the God of heaven know that the struggle can be physically and emotionally exhausting; for to wrestle with God is to question his methods and fairness, to doubt his justice and mercy, and even to blame him for the immeasurable difficulties that life can bring. Moreover, to contend with God is to argue with him, to become angry with him, and even to insist that he is anything but a loving, caring God. Those of us who wrestle with God shout at him. We sometimes turn away from him. At times, we even throw up our hands and wonder if he exists at all. Yet, these painful thoughts and emotions are part of the wilderness encounter with God.

Therefore, the wilderness journey is an invitation to a struggle, and even when we willingly enter the fray, God does not give in to our cries when things become difficult and do not go as we had hoped. Many times God is a firm mentor who allows us to suffer and struggle with the issues of our lives so that we can grow toward spiritual maturity. In fact, God usually leaves us cooking in the fiery oven of life's trials long after we think we are well done. Thus, like Jacob at the ford of the Jabbok, those who wrestle with God often limp away hurt and wounded (Gen. 32:22–32).

HEEDING THE CALL

For many reading this book, the call to the wilderness of change and growth has been clarion clear. Events or circumstances such as divorce, addiction, loss of a job, a debilitating illness, or other painful situations have brought them to the ash pile of life. Now, after having sat in ashes scraping their sores like the biblical Job, they have heard the call and have responded by embarking on the journey into the wilderness of change and growth, wherein they have begun to wrestle with God.

For others, however, the call to the journey may be less clear and may come in subtler, less obvious forms than the painful circumstances just described. These incipient pilgrims begin to faintly hear the call when they start to notice an uneasy restlessness in their hearts, a stirring deep within. They no longer feel at peace with themselves. They become increasingly unhappy, perhaps even depressed, about their current situation. Their loved ones begin to notice their distress and tell them so. Finally, their familiar misery becomes unbearable because they know in their hearts they are not doing what God has created them to do.

Moreover, they begin to experience stress, depression, and burnout—common markers that identify the need for a passport to the wilderness. According to author Sam Keen:

> Stress . . . is a symptom that you are living somebody else's life, marching to a drumbeat that doesn't syncopate with your personal body rhythms, playing a role you didn't create, living a script written by an alien authority. Depression . . . is a distant early warning that you are on the wrong path and that something in you is being pressed down, beat on, kept imprisoned, dishonored. Burnout is nature's way of telling you you've been going through the motions but your soul has departed; you're a zombie, a member of the walking dead, a sleepwalker.[1]

Stress, depression, and burnout are maladies that plague those restless spiritual pilgrims who have remained past their time in the village compound—that is, in the realm of safety, security, certainty, and, all too commonly, spiritual vacuity. To grow spiritually, they must leave the stifling, sleep-inducing air of the village, slip beyond its gates, and venture into the fresh air of the thinly populated wilderness.

For most of us, however, the problem is not in knowing when God is calling us beyond the village walls; the problem is having the faith to strike out on our own. Because we so often lack faith, we refuse to listen to the quiet, internal stirring of the divine voice or to hear it speaking through those who truly are our friends. Rather than pay attention, we go into denial: we pretend that we do not hear what we hear; we put on the headphones and turn up the Walkman. Perhaps we stay busy so that we cannot hear that still, small voice of God: we clean the house or throw ourselves into our work, hoping that God will leave us alone. Or maybe we decide to sleep in. Perhaps we get involved in yet another relationship to keep our thoughts occupied so that we do not have to hear God's call to that threatening wilderness journey. Perhaps we simply pop open another can of beer or take out the chocolate marble ice cream. To be sure, there are many ways to refuse the call to the wilderness of change and growth.

Nevertheless, those among us who dare to go forth by faith must remember that to reach the land flowing with milk and honey, we must leave the safety and security of the village and journey into the unknown, dragon-haunted wilderness of change and growth, wherein we may encounter and be transformed by the living God. Gold is not dug in the village; gold is dug in lonely, solitary, unseen places. In these uninhabited regions, God quietly transforms our ashes into gold.

Abraham, Father of the Faithful

Those who embark upon the wilderness journey follow the example of our spiritual forefather Abraham, the foremost patriarch of the Hebrews. Because he so deeply trusted God, Abraham is known as the father of the faithful.

The patriarch Abraham was a man of considerable wealth and influence in Haran, his homeland. He possessed vast properties, great herds of livestock, many servants, and the various other accoutrements of the wealthy. No doubt he wielded considerable social and political influence in his native land as well. Were he living today, we would describe him as the embodiment of the American dream. He had it made; he was set for life in his comfortable existence in Haran. But God, who had other plans for Abraham, interrupted his idyllic existence and called him to leave the secure, familiar surroundings of his village and journey to a strange, unknown land, wherein God would fulfill a divine plan through him. The Scriptures tell us: "By faith Abraham, when called to go to a place he would later receive as his inheritance, obeyed and went, *even though he did not know where he was going*" (Heb. 11:8, emphasis added). Abraham, the man of faith, obeyed God's call to the wilderness journey and left his country, even though he did not know where he was going (Gen. 12:1ff).

No doubt many of us (myself included) shudder at the prospect of leaving our secure, familiar surroundings and embarking on a journey whose destination is unknown. Yet there come times in the life of each spiritual pilgrim when we must leave that which is comfortable and familiar and journey to those strange, unknown, and, often, lonely places to which God calls us. Like Abraham, many of us are called to leave without knowing where we are going.

Therefore, to venture into the unknown, unfamiliar wilderness of change and growth requires a willingness to open ourselves to outcomes and to live with the inherent uncertainties of the spiritual journey. As we have seen, there is no map to guide us easily through this wilderness. Like the Israelites of old who journeyed day by day beneath the pillar of cloud, we journey one day at a time under the guidance of God, and we rarely know what awaits us around the next bend.

The true path, then, is the insecure path. There are no guarantees on the wilderness journey, no assurances that we will arrive at the promised land unscathed, uninjured, or otherwise unharmed. Remember that this is the arena wherein we wrestle with God, and in such a place, we will be wounded. Our selfish, demanding egos will be shattered as we die to self in the encounter with our heavenly mentor. Those who seek guarantees of security and assurances of safety need not apply for passports to the wilderness of change and growth. Rather, they must remain in the village where it is safe, secure, and spiritually stifling.

A Modern Pilgrim

Because the prospects of venturing forth with no assurances are indeed frightening, perhaps we should take courage from the example of a modern pilgrim who has journeyed into the uncharted wilderness before us.

In my city lives a gifted and talented ballerina named Kathy Thibodeaux. She was the silver medalist in the prestigious Second International Ballet Competition. As a result of her great success in that event, Ms. Thibodeaux achieved international recognition as a ballerina, and a promising future as an artist in a prestigious dance troupe awaited her. God, however, chose to change the direction of her blossoming career by calling her to use the gift of dance he had given her as a witness for him. Therefore, in 1986, "with no dancers or money, and no office or studio space, Kathy resigned her position with the local ballet company to begin Ballet Magnificat," a company of Christian artists who proclaim through dance the gospel of the Lord Jesus Christ.[2]

Ms. Thibodeaux's actions were clearly contrary to popular wisdom. No doubt, many assured her that she was unwise to begin such an enterprise without money, dancers, or studio space. Very likely, she was told that she was mistaken to resign her position in the local ballet company. Popular wisdom tells us to cover our bases, to make plans, to figure it all out before we make a life-changing move. According to popular wisdom, before we begin a vastly new and different enterprise, we should have a couple of aces up our sleeves: we should have money or, at least, financial backing; we should have a place in which to carry out our plans; we should have a plan B to fall back on if things do not go our way. Kathy Thibodeaux had none of these things. However, she did have three things that were necessary for her journey: 1) she had a vision, 2) she had talent, and, 3) most importantly, she had faith. Fortunately for the many who have been blessed by the witness of Ballet Magnificat, Ms. Thibodeaux did not adhere to popular wisdom. Instead, like Abraham, she set out on a journey, even though she could not see where she was going.

Since its founding in 1986, Ballet Magnificat has given hundreds of performances throughout the United States and Canada. They have received invitations from all over the world to travel as missionaries of dance. The company has grown to include choreographers and other staff, and they have opened a school to train dancers in a Christian atmosphere. They also offer summer workshops that attract dancers from across the country.[3]

As we look at the history of Ballet Magnificat, we can see plainly that God was involved in the project from the beginning. Hindsight, of course, is much better than foresight—and also much easier. Years ago, when Kathy Thibodeaux was wrestling with God over the divine will for her life, no doubt the future seemed unsure and frightening. The pursuit of a conventional career as a ballet artist would surely have seemed an easier, softer way. Yet when God is at work, conventionality and popular wisdom fall by the wayside. Moreover, the journey to which God calls us is *not* an easier, softer way; rather, it is a journey of dying to the old so that we may be reborn to the new; it is a journey of letting go of what we cling to so that God may fill our empty hands with the good things he desires for us; it is a journey of leaving the comfortable and familiar and entering the strange and dry places wherein God transforms us according to the divine plan.

THE BACK PARTS OF GOD

Those who journey by faith into the wilderness of change and growth will face many difficulties. Time and again they will confront the awful dragons, Fear and Desire. Moreover, they will be plagued by uncertainty and doubt. Because the journey of spirituality is hard and fraught with perils, they will need to turn again and again to God for reassurance.

Even Moses, the human leader of the wandering Israelites, sought reassurance that God was with him and the people in his charge. Although he had received his mission directly from God, who spoke to him from the burning bush on Mount Horeb; although he had witnessed the cataclysmic plagues that God brought upon Egypt; although he had seen the waters of the Red Sea part before his upheld staff, Moses still sought reassurance that God was with him and his fellow Israelites.

On one memorable occasion, when the people were still camped at the base of Mount Sinai, Moses earnestly beseeched God to make his presence known. Because he lacked the confidence that God was with him and the people, he wanted reassurance. When he came before God in the tent of meeting, a place where he often spoke with God (Ex. 33:7–11), Moses prayed, "If your presence does not go with us, do not send us from here. How will anyone know that you are pleased with me and with your people unless you go with us? What else will distinguish me and your people from all the other people on the face of the earth?" (Ex. 33:15–16). Moses finally made plain his pressing need for reassurance when he said to God, "Now show me your glory" (v. 18).

God responded to Moses' request, but undoubtedly not exactly as Moses had hoped. God said:

> I will do the very thing you have asked. . . . There is a place
> near me where you may stand on a rock. When my glory
> passes by, I will put you in a cleft in the rock and cover you
> with my hand until I have passed by. Then I will remove my
> hand and *you will see my back*; but my face must not be seen.
> (Ex. 33:17, 21–23; emphasis added)

We must not fail to understand the symbolic meaning of God's response to Moses' request. Moses wanted direct assurance that God was with him on his mission to lead the people of Israel through the wilderness to the Promised Land; thus, he asked God to reveal his glory. God, however, did not appear to Moses face to face; instead, he showed Moses only his back.

According to theologian Alister McGrath, Moses is denied a vision of the face of God—that is, a revelation of God recognizable as God—and instead is granted a real, but not necessarily recognizable, revelation of God.[4] In other words, Moses did not see God in the manner that he expected. He did not receive a revelation of God that was clearly recognizable as God; nevertheless, what he received *was* a revelation of the divine. God was there, though not in the manner Moses expected.

Like Moses, we expect God to behave in a certain way. We want God to respond to our situations, especially the painful ones, in a particular manner. We want God to behave according to the dictates of our desires. If we are deeply honest with ourselves, we may need to admit that we want to be god in the place of God and reduce the Creator to a cosmic puppet whose strings we control.

Moses clearly had an expectation of how God should respond to his request; he naively expected to see God in all the divine glory. But, as author Pat Morley has written, "There is a God we want, and there is a God who is—and they are not the same."[5] Thus Moses did not get the god he wanted; he got the God who is! God came to Moses on God's terms, not on Moses' terms. God chose to show Moses only his back. Thus, Moses received a revelation of God that was not clearly recognizable as God. Moses saw God from behind. The view was obscure; it was unclear; yet, it was God.

God does not directly appear to us today anymore than he did to Moses centuries ago. God does not send us apocalyptic signs from heaven to direct our paths. For reasons that probably no one can answer in a totally satisfactory manner, God chooses to remain shrouded in mystery. God's reasons for doing so, however, must, in some way, be connected to the divine wish that those of us who seek to live a genuinely spiritual life place our faith and trust in the divine process that undergirds our lives. Were God to appear to us directly, face to face, and clearly state a list of divine commands and intentions for our lives, there would, of course, be no room for faith. Instead, God remains in what an unidentified Christian mystic of the Middle Ages called a "cloud of unknowing." We may sense the divine presence, we can even know that God is with us, but our knowing must always be enshrouded in a cloud of mystery whose foggy thickness can only be penetrated by faith.

If we would please God, we must live by faith and not by sight (2 Cor. 5:7), for it is in the seeming uncertainty—the unknowing—that we come to know the God who is rather than the god we want. It is through God's apparent absence that we learn truly to trust in the divine presence. Faith is being certain of that which comes to us in uncertainty. It is an assurance of that which is unseen just as though it were seen (Heb. 11:1). Now is not the time for seeing face to face; that time is yet to come. Now, we cannot see God directly or always know the divine will clearly. Now, like Moses, we see only the back parts of God. In the daily events of our lives, God often remains obscure, mysterious, "a poor reflection as in a mirror" (1 Cor. 13:12). And we must live with that—by faith.

Feeling Forsaken

Professor James Atkinson writes, "God tells Moses that he shall never see his face, only his back: and that is his only certainty. [Martin] Luther interprets 'the back parts of God' to mean the despair and the anguish of the absence of God, of being forsaken by God, of the contradictions of life."[6]

Nowhere, of course, is the apparent absence and obscurity of God so evident as in Jesus' cruel and agonizing death on a rough, Roman cross, so graphically and clearly portrayed in Mel Gibson's film, *The Passion of the Christ*. We must remember that "Christianity has its roots in a moment of supreme darkness, as Christ hung dying at Calvary."[7] In that horrible, humiliating scene, God seemed totally absent. How could such a despicable event have occurred if God were involved? Surely the heavenly Father must have been far away when Jesus uttered his cry of dereliction, "My God, my God, why have you forsaken me?" (Matt. 27:46).

Those disciples who witnessed Jesus' last gasp of breath on that fateful Friday descended into the depths of despair as their hopes and dreams were dashed to the ground and crushed underfoot by the oppressive Roman government. Like their crucified friend and leader, they, too, must have felt forsaken by God.

Like Jesus, and like those first Christians who witnessed his merciless and agonizing death on the cross at Calvary, we, too, may feel forsaken by God. This at times overwhelming sense of abandonment contributes heavily to the pain and longing that sometimes characterize the life of faith, for there can be much pain and longing in faith. Although by the exercise of faith, belief and trust may become easier, the life of faith is not always easy. Well meaning friends tell us, "Just trust the Lord, and everything will be all right." To be sure, they are correct in what they are saying; but the glib manner in which such words often are spoken denies or overlooks the pain, anguish, and uncertainty that sometimes accompany the life of faith. To trust God is right; yet, it is also right to admit that such trust is not always easy or casual. Though trust is never blind, it is, nevertheless, trust in something unseen, and it can be very tenuous and unsure.

Many of our days lack what may seem on other, brighter days to be clear evidence that we are on the path God intends us to travel. To be sure, there are occasional signs along the way—usually small ones that have meaning only to us and those closest to us—that enliven us with hope and reassure us that we are traveling the divinely appointed path. The distance between even these small, intimate signs, however, is often so great that we grow increasingly hungry and thirsty as we journey from signpost to signpost. Our hunger and thirst are painful. Like those who struggle for breath, we feel aching deep within our chests. We gasp; we ask God to infuse us with life-giving hope, some symbolic token of the divine presence in our lives. "Anything God," we plead, "just give me some kind of sign that I am doing what you want me to do. Please let me know that you are with me, God!" The more honest among us will admit that in these painful and uncertain times, doubt is a familiar companion on our journeys.

So often God remains distant and aloof, or so it seems from our very limited viewpoint. "Why won't you answer, God?" our pleading goes on. "Where are you? Why won't you show the way?" While we long to travel in the brightness of the divine presence, instead, we grope in the darkness of unknowing, as often as not uncertain that we are traveling in the right direction. We hurt, we cry out, yet God seems to remain distant. The divine messenger bearing the waxed and sealed orders of the king does not appear.

The Way of the Cross

Yet, herein we come again to the central message of Christianity, for the central theme of our faith is not resurrection and glory, but the cross: the pain, the agony, the frustration, the despair, the dying—and, yes, eventually the glory. But we must go through the pain before we reach the glory. That is the nature of our faith, that is the journey to which we are called. Such is the anguish of seeing only the back parts of God. The longed-for certainty must always be shrouded in uncertainty and a measure of obscurity. Were it any other way, we could not journey in faith—and without faith, it is impossible to please God (Heb. 11:6a). We must travel the way of the cross—the way of the pain, agony, and despair—but always with the hope nested in faith that the road that leads past the cross is also the road that continues to the glory. With the apostle Paul, we must tenaciously cling to the belief that the sufferings of this present life "are not worth comparing with the glory that will be revealed in us" (Rom. 8:18).

Today may find us in despair. Like Jesus nailed in agony to the cross on that bleak Friday two thousand years ago, we may wonder why God seemingly has forsaken us. Today may find us living in darkness and obscurity, the ground uncertain beneath our feet, just as on the day of Christ's death. Today, the weight of the pain of a broken relationship may nearly crush us; the habitual use of alcohol or drugs may imprison us; an obsession with a person or thing may torment us; the loss of a loved one may shred the fabric of our souls; failing health or the loss of a career may leave us in despair; and for many others, the poor choices and mistakes of the past may haunt us. But our despair, suffering, and pain—like the crucifixion—must always be viewed in the light of the following resurrection, vindication, and glory. As Alister McGrath so eloquently states: "The transformation of that darkness into light, as Good Friday gave way to Easter Day, constitutes the basis of the Christian hope—that the dark night of faith will finally give way to the dawn of the resurrection life. But in the meantime we struggle on in the twilight world of faith."[8] Or, in the immortal words of Tony Compolo, "It's Friday, but Sunday's comin'!"[9]

NOT AROUND, BUT THROUGH

Like the Israelites of old, all who enter the wilderness of change and growth must undergo a period of trial and testing, a heated time when God refines us in the fire of spiritual transformation. Those who wish to grow psychologically, emotionally, and, especially, spiritually cannot circumvent the harsh wilderness of change and growth. If we are to grow, we must go through the pain; we cannot go around it. There is, in fact, no easier, softer way to the land flowing with milk and honey. If we are to experience joy and contentment, as well as the peace that transcends all understanding, we must undergo the fiery and transforming heat of the wilderness experience. We must remain in the oven until we are well done. This is the meaning of the Exodus story, the saga of all who journey from Egypt to the promised land.

THE TRANSFORMING POWER OF GOD'S LOVE

And we know that in all things God works for the good of those who love him, who have been called according to his purpose.
(Rom. 8:28)

We have seen that God called the Israelites out of the ashes of harsh slavery and bondage in Egypt. God led them across the threshold at the Red Sea and then beyond into the wilderness of change and growth. The Israelites were not able to enter the Promised Land, however, because they were spiritual children. They needed a lengthy time of trial and testing to mold them into a unique people among the nations of the earth.

After forty years of wandering in the wilderness of change and growth, the Israelites did, in fact, enter the Promised Land, where they drove out its pagan inhabitants and established a unique nation (Jos. 1:1ff). The history of that nation is unlike that of any other, for in no other place at any time has God so actively participated in the affairs of humankind. From its humble beginnings in slavery, Israel became the dominant nation of the earth under the rule of Solomon, the wisest man and wealthiest king of the ancient world, and the builder of the legendary temple of God. During Solomon's reign, Israel was the most powerful kingdom on earth; Jerusalem, its capital, the world's most beautiful city; and the temple the most magnificent building anywhere.[10] Truly, the Hebrews saw their ashes turned into gold.

Like the ancient Israelites, God may call into the wilderness those he seeks to transform and refine. Quite often, the divine invitation to change and growth may come to those who weep because everything they hold dear lies in ashes at their feet. Perhaps *your* life is in ashes as a result of the slavery of alcohol or drug abuse; or, you may sit alone in the ash pile and weep as a result of years of abuse and cruel mistreatment. Perhaps your ashes are the result of an unwanted and heartbreaking divorce; or, you may hold only a handful of ashes as the leftovers of a career ruined by economic or political circumstances beyond your control. Perhaps you have lost a loved one or have been diagnosed with a debilitating illness. To be sure, there are many ways to travel the painful path that Robert Bly called "the road of ashes, descent, and grief."[11] That road is a path of tears, a way of pain and suffering that often seems unending to those who trudge it. Nonetheless, it is a road that many must travel to reach the land flowing with milk and honey. As you embark on the path that leads from your place of ashes, your experience will mirror that of the wandering Hebrews as they left the bondage of Egypt. Near the beginning of your journey, you will come to a threshold, a place or time of reckoning that must be crossed if you are to enter the wilderness of change and growth. Like the Israelites who arrived at the shore of the Red Sea, you will encounter at your moment of decision the dragon of fear, daring you not to venture out of your familiar misery. Its awful roar will tempt you mightily to turn back, yet the way to the promised land lies beyond. Do not go backwards; instead, march forward by faith into the teeth of the dragon. Just as God was with the Hebrews as they stepped into the sea, God will be with you. Take courage from the words of the psalmist David: "Even though I walk through the valley of the shadow of death, I will fear no evil, for you are with me; your rod and your staff, they comfort me" (Ps. 23:4).

No sooner will you have gone past the dragon of fear than the dragon of desire will attempt to lure you from the path. That protean beast will appear in a disguise designed especially for you, for it knows what you think you want, and it will promise it to you. Do not be deceived by its seductive glance or its siren song. Though it promises the moon, it will deliver only more ashes.

Remember that the Temple of Life in the middle of the garden lies beyond both Fear and Desire. To be sure, you will confront these dragons not only once, but many times on the path. They may even grow larger and more powerful, but if you stay the course, your shield of faith will grow stronger and more powerful as well. By faith, you will get past Fear and Desire again and again.

The greatest danger, however, will be your own selfish, demanding ego. His majesty the baby—that innately selfish, manipulative, and demanding aspect of human nature—will rise from the grave and threaten to pull you under time and again. You will grow discontent with the way God manages your affairs, and you will be tempted to jerk the reins from the divine hands and take control once more. But remember that as you journey through the wilderness of change and growth, you must surrender your will and your life to God every day; you must die daily.

As you continue your journey, take heart in knowing that, even though the path is hot, dry, and you grow thirsty, God will provide the occasional oasis, though it may appear sometime after what you thought were the limits of your endurance. Also, you will discover not only the timely shady grove, but even the occasional desert rose hidden among the thorns. Moreover, you will likely meet a few other wandering pilgrims who will walk a little way with you and help you on your journey.

I encourage those of you who have experienced the ashes of life to embark upon the journey of spirituality through the wilderness of change and growth. Do not fall short of the mark by settling for the crumbs of Egypt; wait for the feast, and trust that it will be worth it. I urge you to stay the course as you undergo the trials and hardships of the wilderness experience. Do not be like the tired soldier who thought of returning to hell though nothing awaited him but a shovel and more ashes. Do not look back, even though the temptation to do so will be common. Remain in the sparse and uninhabited regions until God calls you out, until the work is done, and you have been transformed into the unique person God would have you become. Finally, like the soldier in the fairy tale who reached his hand into one of the bags of ashes he carried, you, too, will discover that God has turned your ashes into gold!

Notes

Introduction

This original story is loosely based on an idea in the Grimm Brothers' tale "The Devil's Grimy Brother," in Jakob and Wilhelm Grimm, *Grimms' Tales for Young and Old*, trans., Ralph Manheim (New York: Anchor Books, 1977), 349–352.

Chapter 1

[1] Robert Bly, *Iron John: A Book About Men* (Reading, Massachusetts: Addison-Wesley Publishing Company, Inc., 1990), 79.

[2] John Keller, "Pain, Brokenness, and Human Limitation," in *Let Go, Let God* (Minneapolis: Augsburg Publishing House, 1985), 13–17. This elegant and poignant phrase is used several times in the present book.

[3] While I do not believe that the descent into ashes is absolutely essential for spiritual transformation to begin, I do believe that, for many of us, it is necessary.

[4] *Alcoholics Anonymous Comes of Age* (Carmichael, CA: A.A. Publishing, Inc., 1957), 63–64.

[5] Ibid.

[6] Charles Colson, *Loving God* (Grand Rapids: Zondervan Publishing House, 1983), 24–25.

Chapter 2

[1] Morton Kelsey, *Myth, History, and Faith: The Mysteries of Christian Myth and Imagination* (Rockport, Massachusetts: Element, Inc., 1991), 00.

[2] Bly, *Iron John*, 56–91.

Chapter 3

[1] My description of the Temple of Life is based on material in Joseph Campbell, *Reflections on the Art of Living: A Joseph Campbell Companion*, Selected and Edited by Diane K. Osbon (New York: HarperCollins Publishers, 1991), 143–145.

Chapter 4

[1] George MacDonald, *365 Readings*, Edited and with a Preface by C.S. Lewis (New York: Collier Books, 1986), 33.

[2] John F. MacArthur, *The MacArthur New Testament Commentary: Matthew 1–7* (Chicago: Moody Press, 1985), 420.

[3] Ibid., 419.

[4] Ibid.

[5] William Barclay, *The Gospel of Matthew*, vol. 1, The Daily Study Bible (Philadelphia: The Westminster Press, 1956), 261.

[6] MacDonald, *365 Readings*, 33.

[7] Barclay, *Matthew*, 261.

[8] Martin M. Davis, *The Gospel and the Twelve Steps* (Enumclaw, WA: Pleasant Word, 2004). Available at www. ashesintogold.com.

[9] Billy Graham, *Peace with God* (Waco, TX: Word Books, 1984), 134. In Davis, *The Gospel and the Twelve Steps*.

Chapter 5

[1] John R. Claypool, *Opening Blind Eyes* (Nashville: Abingdon Press, 1983; Oak Park, IL: Meyer-Stone Books, 1987), 13.

[2] The Book of Exodus, chapters twenty through thirty-one, contains the lengthy list of laws and instructions that God gave to Moses. Recorded there are the Ten Commandments, as well as rules and regulations regarding the treatment of servants, personal injuries, protection of property, social responsibility, and Sabbath regulations. Also recorded there are detailed instructions both for the building of a tabernacle and for making the garments for the priests who would someday serve in it. When God had finished revealing these laws, Moses was

given "two tablets of the Testimony, the tablets of stone inscribed by the finger of God" (Ex. 31:18).

³ Gerald G. May, *Addiction and Grace* (San Francisco: HarperCollins, 1991), 21.

⁴ I constructed this picturesque description of the dragon of desire from a phrase originally developed by Joseph Campbell.

⁵ Richard J. Foster, "The Dark Side of Money," in *Money, Sex and Power: The Challenge of the Disciplined Life* (San Francisco: Harper & Row, Publishers, 1985), 19.

⁶ May, *Addiction and Grace*, 32.

⁷ Eugene Pascal, *Jung To Live By* (New York: Warner Books, Inc., 1992), 65.

⁸ Foster, *Money, Sex and Power*, 25–26. The material in this paragraph about the power of money, and Jesus' teaching regarding it, is from Foster.

⁹ Claypool, *Opening Blind Eyes*, 34.

¹⁰ Alister E. McGrath, *Studies in Doctrine: Justification by Faith* (Grand Rapids: Zondervan Publishing House, 1997), 413–414.

¹¹ MacDonald, *365 Readings*, 10.

¹² McGrath, *Studies in Doctrine*, 433.

[13] St. Augustine, *Confessions*, quoted in W. Neil, ed., *Concise Dictionary of Religious Quotations*, (Grand Rapids: William B. Eerdmans, 1974), 60.

[14] C.S. Lewis, *The Weight of Glory* (San Francisco: HarperSanFrancisco, 2001), 30–31.

Chapter 6

[1] Though he was not a Christian, Joseph Campbell was a devoted student of the world's spiritual traditions. He had an admirable ability to encapsulate universal spiritual truths in short, pithy statements, as the opening words to the present chapter demonstrate. Unfortunately, I have been unable to locate the source of this statement.

[2] In Matthew 6:34, the original Greek carries the connotation, "Take no *anxious* thought about tomorrow." Thus, the translators of the New International Version render the phrase, "Do not worry about tomorrow."

[3] Robert M. Doran, "Jungian Psychology and Christian Spirituality: III," in *Carl Jung and Christian Spirituality*, ed. Robert L. Moore (New York: Paulist Press, 1988), 100.

[4] For more information about the Dwelling Place, visit the web site at *http://www.dwellingplace.com*, or write to: The Dwelling Place, 2824 Dwelling Place Road, Brooksville, MS 39739.

[5] McGrath, *Studies in Doctrine*, 412.

[6] Ibid., 432.

[7] Ibid., 412.

[8] Ibid., 413

[9] *The International Bible Commentary with the New International Version,* rev. ed., F.F. Bruce, ed. (Grand Rapids: Zondervan, 1986), 1449.

[10] Ibid.

[11] Doran, in *Carl Jung and Christian Spirituality,* 100.

[12] Ibid.

[13] Keller, *Let Go, Let God,* 35.

[14] Ibid., 44.

[15] Ibid., 37.

[16] Ibid., 53.

[17] This sentence is a variation of an original statement from the comparative mythologist Joseph Campbell.

[18] Keller, *Let Go, Let God,* 53.

[19] Ibid., 45.

[20] MacDonald, *365 Readings,* 31.

[21] *Alcoholics Anonymous,* 3d ed. (New York: Alcoholics Anonymous World Services, Inc., 1976), 63.

Chapter 7

[1] Sam Keen, *Fire in the Belly* (New York: Bantam Books, 1991), 147.

[2] Taken from the program of a performance of Ballet Magnificat given in Jackson, MS, at Christmas, 1992 (italics added).

[3] Ibid.

[4] Alister E. McGrath, *The Mystery of the Cross* (Grand Rapids: Academie Books/Zondervan Publishing House, 1988), 105.

[5] Patrick M. Morley, *I Surrender* (Brentwood, TN: Wolgemuth & Hyatt, Publisher, 1990), 5.

[6] James Atkinson, "Forward" in McGrath, *The Mystery of the Cross*, 8.

[7] McGrath, *The Mystery of the Cross*, 113.

[8] Ibid.

[9] Tony Compolo, *It's Friday, But Sunday's Comin'* (Dallas: Word Publishing, 1984), 120.

[10] Henry H. Halley, *Halley's Bible Handbook: An Abbreviated Bible Commentary*, 24th ed. (Grand Rapids: Zondervan Publishing House, 1965), 191.

[11] Bly, "The Road of Ashes, Descent, and Grief," in *Iron John*, 56–91.

To order
additional copies of this book

or

for information on seminars, telephone and e-mail
counseling, or weekend retreats

please visit author's secure web site at:

www.ashesintogold.com

or send $13.95* each book plus $3.00 S&H** to:

Manna Books & Counseling Ministry
PO Box 16354
Jackson, MS 39236–6354

*MS residents, add 7% sales tax
**add $1.00 S&H for each additional book ordered

You may also order this book directly
from the publisher.
Have your credit card ready and call

Toll free: (877) 421-READ (7323)
or
order online at: www.winepressbooks.com